MAFEKING
1899–1900

EXPLORE HISTORY'S MAJOR CONFLICTS WITH
BATTLE STORY

MAFEKING
1899–1900

EDMUND YORKE

First published 2014 by
Spellmount, an imprint of
The History Press
The Mill, Brimscombe Port
Stroud, Gloucestershire, GL5 2QG
www.thehistorypress.co.uk

British Library Cataloguing in Publication Data.
A catalogue record for this book is available from the British Library.

ISBN 978 0 7509 5566 9

Typesetting and origination by The History Press
Printed in Great Britain

CONTENTS

ACKNOWLEDGEMENTS

Several friends and colleagues have made valuable contributions to this work. Firstly, I wish to especially thank Colonel Malcolm Flower-Smith (retired), my co-researcher and expert in this area, who has supplied key source material in the past, notably the Algie Diary, and some of the quotes enclosed in this work. Secondly, Curator Audrey Renew, who over a decade ago kindly loaned much primary source material from the Mafikeng Archives, notably the Algie Diary. Thirdly, the late Betty Clay CBE, daughter of Lord Baden-Powell, who provided great inspiration and encouragement for this and previous works. Fourthly, Colonel Ian Bennett (retired), military historian and author of the outstanding book *The Siege of Potchefstroom*, who also provided source material for the new logistical perspective on this siege. My old Cambridge colleague Bill Nasson's splendid book *The South African War* and his numerous articles greatly stimulated my thoughts on the racial implications arising from the conduct of this siege, as did Thomas Pakenham's masterly general study of this fascinating conflict. I would also like to thank senior librarian Andrew Orgill and his two assistants, John Pearce and Ken Franklin, of the Royal Military Academy, Sandhurst (RMAS) Library for their usual unfailing assistance in securing rare books and manuscripts. Above all, I would like to thank my family, especially my wife, Louise, for her word-processing support, and daughters,

Madeleine and Emily, for their great forbearance during the long gestation of this project.

The main aim of this book is to use revised and updated primary source material, drawn mainly from my extensive published and unpublished research on the Anglo-Boer War, as well as that of several selected leading experts, to present, for both specialists and non-specialists, a clear and hopefully balanced and concise analysis of this epic, if still controversial, siege.

The opinions expressed in this work are my own and do not reflect those of either the Ministry of Defence or the Royal Military Academy, Sandhurst.

INTRODUCTION

I feel assured that Her Majesty's Government will agree with me in thinking that the utmost credit is due to Major-General Baden-Powell ... for the resolution, judgement and resource which he displayed throughout the long and trying investment of Mafeking by the Boer Forces. The distinction which Major-General Baden-Powell has earned must be shared by his gallant soldiers. No episode in the present war seems more praiseworthy than the prolonged defence of this town by a British garrison, consisting almost entirely of Her Majesty's Colonial forces, inferior in numbers and greatly inferior in artillery to the enemy, cut off from communication with Cape Colony, and with the hope of relief repeatedly deferred until the supplies of food were nearly exhausted.

Field Marshal Roberts to the Secretary of State for War, Commander-in-Chief South Africa, Pretoria, 21 June 1900

* * *

I saw them fall down on the veldt and lie where they had fallen, too weak to go on their way. The sufferers were mostly little boys – mere infants ranging from four to five upwards… Hunger had them in its grip and many of them were black spectres and living skeletons … their ribs literally breaking their shrivelled skin – men, women and children. Probably hundreds died from starvation or disease that always accompanies famine. Certain it is that many were found dead on the veldt.

Neilly, *Besieged with BP*, pp. 227–9 (Yorke and Flower-Smith, *Mafeking*, p. 120)

***

It is understood that you have armed Bastards, Fingos and Baralongs against us – in this you have committed an enormous act of wickedness … reconsider the matter, even if it cost you the loss of Mafeking … disarm your blacks and thereby act the part of a white man in a white man's war.

General Cronje to Colonel Baden-Powell, 29 October 1899 (Pakenham, *The Boer War*, p. 396)

***

The siege and battle for Mafeking constitutes one of the most famous, but also one of the most controversial, episodes in British imperial history. Over 217 days, from 13 October 1899 to 17 May 1900, little more than 1,000 totally outgunned and outnumbered European and African defenders, ultimately only surviving on starvation rations and led by Col Baden-Powell, were initially besieged by 8,000 and, from mid-November 1899, a reduced number of around 2,000 Boer fighters, led respectively by Generals Cronje and Snyman. Whilst this epic struggle made a hero out of the British leader, Baden-Powell, who eventually went on to achieve everlasting fame as founder of the Scouting Movement, his personal role has recently attracted criticism for alleged gross neglect of the Mafeking African population, leading to a significant number of unnecessary deaths from starvation.

This study, again deploying primary sources, whilst revisiting and revising the author's and Malcolm Flower-Smith's recent defence of his leadership role, will use new primary sources (recently kindly loaned by historian Col Bennett) to emphasise the chronic logistical imperatives which coloured many of his harsher decisions. There will also be an expanded discussion of the armed African role in the overall defence of Mafeking, especially the opening battles of October/November 1899.

As the quote by Gen. Cronje above graphically exposes, the battle for Mafeking also represented one of the first events of the Anglo-Boer War to highlight the deep racial tensions underpinning this conflict; tensions directly generated by Baden-Powell's equally controversial decision to arm large numbers of his African defenders, which, from the Boer perspective, constituted a gross violation of the sacred principle of fighting a 'white man's war'. Therefore, it was a battle which presented a major challenge to the existing pre-war social order, whereby a white South African minority sought to sustain, in wartime as well as in peacetime, their coercive dominance over a black South African majority.

TIMELINE

1652	Dutch occupy Cape region of South Africa
1806	Britain occupies the Cape
1814	Britain annexes the Cape
1830s	Boer communities commence 'Great Trek' away from British control, penetrating deep into the Southern African interior
1843	Natal annexed as a British colony, raising fears of British encirclement
1852 and 1854	Foundation of the independent Boer Republics of the Orange Free State and the Transvaal
1860s	Diamond discoveries in the Orange Free State renews British interest in dominating the region
1875	Lord Carnarvon officially launches South African Confederation policy to secure British control and to reduce costs of her South African possessions
1877	Britain annexes the bankrupt Transvaal Republic, reinforcing Boer fears of British imperial domination

Timeline

1879	The Anglo-Zulu War. After defeats at Isandlwana, Intombe Drift and Hlobane, and major victories at Rorke's Drift, Gingindlovu and Kambula, Britain finally defeats the main Zulu army at Ulundi. The last African obstacle to Confederation is removed
1880–81	Outbreak of the First Anglo-Boer War (1880–81). British suffer a series of defeats, culminating in Majuba Hill
1881–84	The Pretoria and London Conventions; Britain recognises Boer independence
1886	Gold discoveries in the Transvaal reawaken British interest in controlling the Boer Republics
1886–95	Disputes between the Boer Republics and Britain, particularly over the implementation of the 'Uitlander' franchise issue, raises political tensions
1895	Jameson Raid: this failed armed coup, backed by diamond and gold magnates Cecil Rhodes and Alfred Beit, is launched against the Transvaal government, greatly exacerbating tension between Britain and the Boer Republics
1895–99	Political tensions reach crisis point as the new British High Commissioner to South Africa, Sir Alfred Milner, backed by the Colonial Secretary, Joseph Chamberlain, and determined to demonstrate imperial unity and power via the 'Uitlander' issue, directly clashes with President Kruger
1899	British significantly strengthen their forces in South Africa during the spring and summer months

Mafeking 1899–1900

12 October 1899	After the expiry of a two-day Boer ultimatum demanding guarantees of Boer independence and the withdrawal of British troops and reinforcements arriving after 1 June, Boer forces attack, besieging the key British-held towns of Mafeking, Kimberley and Ladysmith
13 October 1899	Siege of Mafeking begins
December 1899	British forces suffer a series of defeats, notably at Colenso, Magersfontein and Stormberg (known as 'Black Week')
February 1900	Lord Roberts occupies Bloemfontein. Kimberley and Ladysmith relieved. Cronje surrenders at Paardeberg
13 May 1900	Mafeking relieved
June 1900	Lord Roberts occupies Pretoria
1901–02	Last 'Bitter-ender' Boer guerrilla campaign is crushed by Roberts and Kitchener's twin policies of the 'blockhouse' and 'concentration camp' system, denying both resources and battle space to the mobile Boer commandos
31 May 1902	Peace of Vereeniging signed; war ends

HISTORICAL
BACKGROUND:
The Origins of War

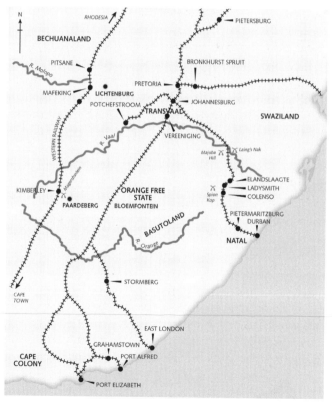

South Africa during the Anglo-Boer War, 1899–1902; key towns and battle sites.

The Anglo-Boer or South African War of 1899–1902 is regarded as the most serious conflict that confronted Britain between the Crimean War and the First World War. Although it primarily represented a struggle between whites for political power, it was equally, as the second title suggests, a war that eventually necessitated, indeed demanded, the participation of local African communities on a large scale. For both Afrikaner white communities and African polities, in particular, it was to prove a time of great hardship and ultimately great suffering. By the end of the almost three-year struggle, nearly 7,000 Boer combatants lay dead, and a further 26,000 to 28,000 Boer civilians, mainly women and children, had perished in the dreaded British 'concentration camps'. The latter tragedy left a bitter legacy of Afrikaner hatred for the British that has lingered on to this day. Twenty-two thousand imperial soldiers also died, the majority from disease. The sheer magnitude or scale of the conflict rapidly became evident as up to 50,000 highly mobile Boer commando fighters faced a massive British imperial army which eventually reached almost half a million men. To this must be added countless Africans who died as innocent civilians or in logistical support roles, and, more controversially, as armed auxiliaries for both sides.

The origins of the Anglo-Boer conflict stretched back for at least a century preceding the outbreak of war in October 1899. While the first substantial Dutch settlement in the area occurred in 1652, it was not until the 1790s that Britain first occupied the area for strategic reasons during the Revolutionary and Napoleonic Wars. Serious friction between the primarily agrarian Afrikaner settlers and their British masters only arose after 1814 when the Cape of Good Hope became a permanent British possession. The steady imposition of British taxes incensed Boer farmers, but it was two particular events that set the scene for future political and military confrontation. The adoption of English as the official language of the colony in 1828 and the 1833 British Parliamentary Act emancipating slaves throughout the British Empire affronted the fiercely independent Boer farming communities. Boer religious beliefs, which rested on strict Calvinism and a perception of African tribal groups as primarily 'hewers of wood and drawers of water', reflecting their economic dependence on slave labour, led many to take the drastic action of literally trekking out of the area, thus physically cutting off links with British authority. The Great Trek of 1836, launched deep into the Southern African interior, led to serious armed clashes with interior African groups, including the crushing defeat of the Zulu armies at Blood River in 1838, all of which further enhanced the generation of a distinct Afrikaner identity and a deep sense of nationhood. However, it was a short-lived freedom. Britain's reaction to the Great Trek – the annexation of Natal in 1843 and the eventual penetration of the area between the Orange and Vaal rivers – only served to resurrect the tension between the recalcitrant Boer farmers and their former imperial masters.

British recognition of Boer independence beyond the Vaal and the Orange rivers (Sand River and Bloemfontein Conventions of 1852 and 1854) reflected a revised British government perception of their limited, political and strategic importance. Again, however, this only proved to be a brief respite for the scattered Boer communities, who increasingly saw themselves as the eternally beleaguered 'white tribe of Africa'. From the late 1850s onwards, pressure to confederate together both the British colonies and these embryonic Afrikaner republics of the Orange Free State and the Transvaal steadily increased, if only to secure the region from the continual internal 'native wars' and thereby reduce local and imperial expenditure.

Economic events provided the final catalyst to direct military clashes between Briton and Boer. The discovery of diamonds in significant quantities during the 1860s revived British interest in the region and the new imperial interventionism was reflected in Lord Carnarvon's attempts to both confederate and ultimately control the whole region under British sovereignty. The twin British annexations of Basutoland (Lesotho) in 1868, after the Free State–Basuto War, and diamond-rich Griqualand West in 1871, reinforced

Afrikaner perceptions of British perfidy and imminent domination. In 1877 the bankruptcy of the Transvaal Republic, itself embroiled in disastrous conflicts with local African tribes, enabled the British to annex this state and further confirm Boer fears.

From 1879 to 1881 military pressures came to the fore as Britain's expansionist frontier policies, rejuvenated under the new South African High Commissioner, Sir Bartle Frere, embroiled Britain in a costly war against the Zulu, the last African obstacle to the grandiose plan of South African confederation. The resultant Pyrrhic victory not only cost the Treasury several million pounds, but also led to a series of devastating military blunders as the British forces initially suffered serious defeats, notably at the battles of Isandlwana and Intombe Drift. Despite the inevitable final elimination of Zulu power at the Battle of Ulundi in July 1879, two years later, the discontented Transvaal Boers, emboldened by these apparent British military weaknesses and supported by their Orange Free State compatriots, rose in revolt. Caught largely by surprise, the often outnumbered British forces in the region suffered a series of setbacks culminating in the humiliating defeat at Majuba Hill in February 1881. To the dismay of many, Gladstone's Liberal government, appalled at the cost of this unexpected war and embarrassed by its political implications, signed the Pretoria Convention (modified by the London Convention of 1884), which granted the Transvaal a limited form of independence.

However, the humiliation of Majuba, combined with the 1886 discovery of rich seams of gold in the Transvaal, ensured that the Boer Republics would never escape the vengeful attentions of the British imperial metropole. As strategic fears escalated, particularly following the enhanced interest of Germany in the region, British pressures became more intense than ever before. In the 1890s control of the alleged pro-German and mineral-rich Transvaal government became a burning imperative. The disastrous 1895 Jameson Raid, an attempted armed coup against the Transvaal, foolishly supported by Cecil Rhodes, Prime Minister of the Cape, who considered that British capital interests in Johannesburg were too great to be left to the mercies of what was perceived to be an inefficient, corrupt and clearly anti-British Kruger government, made war a virtual certainty. British hopes now rested upon the issue of the Uitlander franchise. Following the discovery of gold, the Transvaal had been flooded by foreign miners, predominantly British, and these were known as 'Uitlanders' or outsiders. President Paul Kruger of the Transvaal soon realised their voting power and the direct political threat posed to Boer independence by these white British immigrants. He accordingly proceeded to refuse the extension of citizenship and the franchise, thereby preventing *de facto* British political control of his country. As pressures from the newly appointed and fervently imperialist High Commissioner, Sir Alfred Milner, closely supported in London by Joseph Chamberlain, the Colonial Secretary, massively increased in the closing months of 1899, Kruger, fearing imminent war and aware of the enervated state of British forces in the region, decided to launch a pre-emptive strike. In October 1899, five months after the failure of the Bloemfontein talks between Kruger and Milner, the Transvaal president delivered an ultimatum requiring Britain to immediately cease all overseas troop reinforcements and movement in the region. Britain predictably refused to comply and war broke out on 12 October 1899, with a rapid invasion of Natal by Boer forces and the encirclement of the key strategic centres of Kimberley, Ladysmith and Mafeking.

THE ARMIES

British Forces:
Commanders, Tactics, Kit and Weaponry

The Tactics

At the start of the Second Anglo-Boer war, British tactics were primarily designed to combat 'native enemies' and barely differed from previous colonial wars, such as the recent Sudan (1884–85 and 1897–98) and Afghanistan (1878–80) campaigns. The largely static British Army had learnt little from their reverses of the First Anglo-Boer War (1880–81). 'Waterloo tactics' still prevailed. British line regiments were organised into two-deep ranks, which enabled one rank to kneel or stand to fire and one to load or reload. Square formations for defensive purposes were still religiously taught at Sandhurst, Aldershot and elsewhere in the 1890s. Frontal attacks were still conducted at walking pace with skirmishers dispersed out in front. However, the shock of the 'Black Week' defeats of November/December 1899, notably at Colenso, Magersfontein and Stormberg, belatedly led to tactical innovations with a far greater use of mobile formations, especially mounted infantry units, designed to pin down their elusive and highly mobile Boer enemy. At Mafeking, Baden-Powell was accompanied by only twenty specifically imperial officers and troops; the rest were

S.J.P. (Paul) Kruger (1825–1904)

As the long-term president of the Transvaal, Kruger was the overall Boer political and military leader who confronted the British in the lead-up to the Second Anglo-Boer War. As a 10-year-old boy, Kruger accompanied his parents on the Great Trek. A field cornet at 17, he emerged as the principal Boer leader during the formative years of the Republic. Elected vice-president immediately before the British annexation of the Transvaal in 1877, he led the Triumvirate during the First Anglo-Boer War (1880–81). He was elected president of the Transvaal in 1883, 1888, 1893 and 1898. He fled to Switzerland in 1900 during the Second Anglo-Boer War (1899–1902).

S.J.P. Kruger.

Field Marshal Frederick Sleigh Roberts, Commander-in-Chief South Africa (1832–1914)

As Baden-Powell's superior officer, Roberts played a crucial role in dictating both the logistical and military direction of the siege, and particularly its outside relief operations. Born in Cawnpore, India in 1832, the ageing Roberts had spent most of his service in India, much of it in the Quartermaster branch, and his great reputation was linked to that of the Indian Army. He was the son of a general and he had been awarded a Victoria Cross during the Indian Mutiny. His victories in the Second Anglo-Afghan War (1878–80), especially the relief and Battle of Kandahar, made him the doyen of the British Army and public. After forty-two years' service in India he returned home in 1893 and, in 1895, was promoted to field marshal. In 1900 he was appointed Commander-in-Chief South Africa and both his and Kitchener's ruthless policies of enclosing the open veldt with blockhouse and wire fortifications, alongside farm burning and the enforced transfer and incarceration of Boer families into 'concentration camps', finally reduced the Boers to starvation and surrender. His alleged blunders in the area of logistics and supply, however, which may have delayed relief for Mafeking and elsewhere, remains an area of contention. Roberts died in 1914 on the eve of the First World War while visiting his beloved Indian Contingent in France.

Field Marshal Frederick Sleigh Roberts.

Col Baden-Powell and his military and civil staffs. (Dr E.J. Yorke Collection)

composed of local irregular/volunteer European and European officered African units who, in some significant respects, were better suited to dealing with such an unorthodox enemy.

British Kit

The standard British infantry rifles were the Lee-Metford and the Lee-Enfield, the latter slowly replacing the former and both firing .303 ammunition. Some Metfords were fitted with Enfield barrels as they were refurbished, the rifling being better suited to the cordite ammunition. The colonial units at Mafeking, such as the Bechuanaland Regiment, were issued with Martini-Henry rifles and carbines, many dating back to the 1879 Anglo-Zulu War and the later 1893 and 1896 Mashona/Matabele conflicts in Rhodesia. Some had Martini Metfords or Enfields, which fired the .303 round. Mounted units, such as the Cape Mounted Rifles, had the shorter Lee-Metford or Martini-Henry carbines, later replaced by the Lee-Enfield carbine. Around half of the British garrison at Mafeking were armed with Lee-Metford and half with Martini-Henry rifles.

CHARACTERISTICS OF THE PRINCIPAL RIFLES OF THE OPPOSING SIDES:

Lee-Metford rifle: calibre .303in, muzzle velocity (mv) 1,830 feet per second (fps), sighted to 1,600yd, ten-round magazine, initially black powder, later cordite.
Lee-Metford carbine: as for rifle except with mv 1,680fps, sighted to 1,580yd, six-round magazine.
Martini-Henry rifle: calibre .450in, single-shot, breech-loading (i.e., no magazine), mv approx. 1,500fps, sighted to 1,400yd, black powder.
Mauser: calibre 7mm, mv 2,719fps, sighted to 2,200yd, five-round magazine, smokeless powder.
(Source: Carver, p. 262)

British artillery at Mafeking included four muzzle-loading 7-pounders (lb), an old Hotchkiss 1lb gun, a 2in Nordenfelt and seven .303 Maxim machine guns. Later in the siege these were supplemented by two vintage homemade muzzle-loaders, one an ancient ship's gun, firing a 6lb solid shot, and one constructed in the railway workshops, which fired a 16lb shot up to 4,000yd:

In 1888, Colonel Slade (Rifle Brigade) and Lt-Col Wallace (Kings Royal Rifle Corps) introduced new combat equipment, known as the 'Slade-Wallace' equipment and designed for any climate. It consisted of a waist belt and harness supporting two forty-round ammunition pouches and behind the shoulders, supported by shoulder braces, was a glazed leather valise (bearing the regimental badge) containing field kit and twenty rounds of ammunition. Below the valise hung the mess tin and rolled greatcoat. Crossbelts supported a water canteen on the right hip and a haversack on the left which, when not in use, was rolled into a pad. The bayonet and scabbard were slung on the left side of the belt. In the field, the white Slade-Wallace harness, pouches and haversacks were stained (often

The 'Lord Nelson', an old gun presented to Montsioa, father of Wessels, the Baralong chief. It had lain buried for twenty years, but at the start of the siege was unearthed and handed over to the military by Wessels and used throughout their military operations. (Dr E.J. Yorke Collection)

with tea), as was the standard tropical/pith helmet. All these items matched the now universally adopted khaki dyed trousers and tunic.

When the Anglo-Boer War of 1899–1902 broke out, the British infantry wore the Slade-Wallace equipment with only minor modifications, with the two standard pouches on the front of the body and the mounted infantry wore a fifty-round bandolier. Indeed, the British infantry marched into battle more lightly equipped than ever before, carrying the rolled greatcoat on his waist belt at the back with the mess tin on top and without a valise, a total weight of only 25lb.

Probably only a minority of the Mafeking defenders wore the complete kit described above. With few regulars present and a large number of volunteer colonial units involved, there were a wide variety of uniforms and firearms evident. (Featherstone, pp. 122–6)

Colonel Robert Stephenson Smyth Baden-Powell

Originally named Robert Stephenson Smyth Powell, he was born in 1857, one of fourteen children and the son of a professor of geometry at Oxford University. After his father's premature death when he was aged only 3, his highly ambitious mother changed the family name to the more ostentatiously hyphenated Baden-Powell, with Baden being the more popular first name of her husband's family. After schooling at Charterhouse, where he was already known as 'B-P', and rejection by Balliol and Christ Church Colleges, Oxford University, he opted for the army. However, after passing the entrance exam for the Royal Military College, Sandhurst, he and several others were instead gazetted straight to regiments.

Col Baden-Powell, later Maj. Gen., in his Hussar uniform. (Dr E.J. Yorke Collection)

In Gardner's words, he therefore 'did not have the advantages, or disadvantages, of a formal military education, a fact which never bothered him but which may not be irrelevant to later events'.

As an officer in Lucknow barracks, India from 1879 and attached to the 13th Hussars, he excelled and was known for both his efficiency and reliability, and his sportsmanship and dramatical/musical talent, not least as a great practical joker. Despite his jolly, even frivolous, side he was also remarkably abstemious, nether a drinker nor a smoker. It was in India that he met his lifelong friend, Kenneth McLaren, almost immediately known to fellow officers as 'The Boy' due to his unusually youthful appearance and who fought and died with him in Mafeking. His close friendship with this officer has recently even led to allegations of homosexuality, but other works have noted that Baden-Powell struck up other close friendships with many other military colleagues, e.g. Lt Hazelrigg (who, like McLaren, was also killed during the siege), as part of the normal process of 'military bonding'. (See Flower-Smith and Yorke, *Mafeking*, pp. 18–9)

Baden-Powell's taste and gift for publicity soon earned him the attention of higher authorities. His excellent military maps attracted the attention of the 'Wolseley circle' and his sketches in *The Graphic*, his military manuals and his handbook on 'Reconnaissance and Scouting' were well received. By 1884 he had been promoted to captain and adjutant for his regiment and, as part of reinforcements for the First Anglo-Boer War, he had his first taste of and fell in love with Africa. After postings to the Cape and Malta as ADC to his uncle, Sir Henry Smyth, Baden-Powell joined the Ashanti Expedition in 1895. By April 1896 he had been promoted to brevet lieutenant colonel and took part in the often brutal suppression of the Ndebele (Matabele) Rebellion in Rhodesia. In April 1897 Baden-Powell was given command of the 5th Dragoon Guards in India. It was in July 1899, whilst on his first long leave in England, that he was summoned to see the Commander-in-Chief Lord Wolseley in the War Office and tasked to raise two white settler regiments from Rhodesia and Bechuanaland and, ultimately, in October 1899, to defend the strategically important town of Mafeking on the outbreak of the Second Anglo-Boer War. After the war Baden-Powell proceeded to gain eternal fame by founding, in 1907, the Boy Scout Movement, closely modelled on his Cape Boys formation of the Siege of Mafeking.

The Baden-Powell family. (Dr E.J. Yorke Collection)

Mafeking's artillery. On the extreme right is 'Lord Nelson'. (Dr E.J. Yorke Collection)

The Protectorate Regiment arriving from Ramathlabama before the siege. (Dr E.J. Yorke Collection)

Capt. Marsh, commanding Cape Mounted Police at Mafeking. (Dr E.J. Yorke Collection)

Col Baden-Powell in his South African 'outfit'. (Dr E.J. Yorke Collection)

The Boer Forces:
Commanders, Tactics, Kit and Weaponry

Boer tactics were essentially reflective of their smaller numbers and resources. Using their superior mobility, they were designed to surround and capture key strategic and communication centres, notably Mafeking, Ladysmith and Kimberley, and progressively strangle and disrupt British lines of communication. Costly set-piece battles against the often much larger British formations were generally avoided. Hit and run raids were preferred. It was hoped that, as in the First Anglo-Boer War, British losses of men and material, such as those incurred in 'Black Week', would eventually persuade the British government to sue for peace and thereby preserve Boer independence.

General Piet Cronje (1836–1911)

Cronje was a direct descendant of the Huguenot Pierre Cronier, who arrived in the Cape in 1698. He received some education at Potchefstroom and with his brother, Andries, worked his father's farm, Goedgevonden. He took part in a number of forays against local African tribes and was made a field cornet serving under Kruger. Fiercely opposed to the British annexation of the Transvaal in 1877 he entered public life in 1879 when he was made leader of the Boers in the Potchefstroom district.

As commander of the Transvaal commandos on the western front for the first few weeks of the Mafeking siege, Cronje had already established a reputation for both shrewdness and ruthlessness. Whilst a major participant in the first war with the British (1880–81), he had commanded the significantly unsuccessful Siege of Potchefstroom in 1881, but more recently had greatly enhanced his personal prestige by taking the surrender of the Jameson raiders. Short, ponderous, black-bearded and sharing his president's rough peasant background, 'Honest Piet's' raw courage and buccaneer personality had naturally endeared him to his Transvaal constituents, although his earlier pre-war conviction for torturing Africans under his charge whilst serving as a Native Commissioner testified to the brutal side

Gen. Piet
Cronje.

of his character. His broad strategic plan for his Potchefstroom, Lichtenburg, Marico, Rustenburg and Wolmaransstad commandos was (after joining with Orange Free Staters) to sweep west and south, past Kimberley and on to the Orange River. As a man of truculent and stubborn energy, he intended to firstly brush aside the small garrison of Mafeking, but after only a few weeks in mid-November 1899, he tired of the siege and transferred the bulk of his estimated 8,000 troops to these other fronts, particularly the more valuable prize of Kimberley. The remainder were left to continue to invest the town under the command of his colleague, Gen. J.P. Snyman. His later war record was mixed, with, for example, successes at the battles of Modder River and Magersfontein, but his military reputation suffered severely after his major defeat at Paardeberg in February 1900 by British forces under Gen. Roberts, at which he was forced to surrender a force of over 4,000.

Accompanied by his wife, Cronje was imprisoned on St Helena until the end of the war. Returning home he was ostracised by his fellow Boer compatriots and he travelled to the USA in 1904 to join a show giving dramatised representations of the Boer War. Disenchanted with his reception, he returned home in 1905 to spend his remaining years at Palmietfontein, isolated, lonely and unhappy. (Sources: Gardner, Carver, Pakenham and Bennett)

ASSISTANT COMMANDANT-GENERAL J.P. SNYMAN

The Boer leader who replaced Cronje in mid-November 1899 was also a veteran of past conflicts. His approach to the siege was distinctly different from his more gung-ho superior, Cronje. Commanding the rump of the originally 8,000-stong force, his remaining 2,000-odd men were deployed with greater caution. As Gardner has succinctly observed: 'The Boer system was that the commandants of commandos should elect their own local commanders, but Snyman's election must have been based on deeds of the past rather than hopes for the future: he was not an energetic man and he was known to be over-fond of the bottle.' His great patience was renowned and he opted for steady blockade, his reasoning being that if he could starve the defenders into submission, then all well and good; if he could not, then at least he would secure the entire area for the Republics by safeguarding any danger to Boer communications and flanks from Baden-Powell. Snyman's tactics of extreme caution and his frequent unwillingness to give battle infuriated the far more pro-active and battle-hungry Baden-Powell who, according to Gardner, 'detested the memory of him for the rest of his life'.

(Sources: Gardner, Pakenham)

A Typical Boer Fighter

President Kruger's troops were unique in many ways. Apart from one or two commanders and their largely foreign artillery units, they were barely trained in the traditional military sciences. They were essentially frontiersmen; highly mobile, expert horsemen, crack shots and masters of their largely open veldt terrain. Organised into *commandos* (locally raised detachments of fifty or more men) they wore slouch hats and well-worn bush clothes, with double bandoliers slung over their shoulders and across their chests. They carried a wide variety of firearms, predominantly imported

German magazine-fed Mausers and single-shot Martini-Henry rifles, but were also inclined to deploy captured British Lee-Metford rifles later in the war. Logistically, they were largely self-contained, accompanied by trains of ox-wagons carrying ammunition and stores. Ammunition supply could be a problem and it was not unknown for commandos to follow British detachments later in the war for the sole purpose of collecting cartridges often carelessly dropped by their invariably better-supplied 'Tommy' enemy. Whilst often appearing to be, in military terms, a disorganised rabble, they were proud, stubborn, tough, elusive and highly experienced due to the many previous years of bush warfare. Kipling brilliantly portrayed the typical Boer fighter in a verse of one of his many poems depicting the Anglo-Boer War:

> Ah there Piet! – be'ind 'is stony kop,
> With 'is Boer bread an' biltong, an' 'is flask of awful Dop;
> 'Is Mauser for amusement an' 'is pony for retreat,
> I've known a lot o' fellers shoot a dam' sight worse than Piet.

Maj. Gen. Robert Stephenson Smyth Baden-Powell. (Dr E.J. Yorke Collection)

They were, in Gardner's words, 'in open conditions, the most formidable military exponents in the world'. By the last year of the war, however, their almost total reliance on mobility had become their 'Achilles heel' as the British, under Gens Roberts and Kitchener, ruthlessly and systematically pinned them down and emasculated their supply bases by the combined means of the 'blockhouse' and 'concentration camp' system. (Gardner, Carver, Flower-Smith/Yorke and Kipling, *The Five Nations*, p. 201)

Boer Kit

In 1896 both the Transvaal and the Orange Free State, foreseeing a major conflict, had ordered large quantities of rifles. The Transvaal purchased 50,000 German Mausers from Krupps (although only 37,000 had been delivered by the time the war started) and 34,000 Martini-Henry rifles from Westley Richards. They had also acquired 7,500 Portuguese Guedes and 2,700 Lee-Metfords, some of which they had captured from Jameson after his infamous raid of 1895. The Orange Free State ordered 18,000 Mausers, of which only 8,000 had been delivered by 1899. They also had Martini-Henrys and Lee-Metfords supplied to them by the Transvaal (Carver, p. 261). At Mafeking, the majority of the besieging Boer forces would have been issued with Mauser rifles.

The Boer artillery units represented their only true professional force. The Free State Artillery was established in 1880, while the Transvaal State Artillery was set up ten years later in 1890. Significant numbers of well-trained foreign volunteer gunners were also employed alongside trained locals. At Mafeking, Gen. Cronje was equipped with a significant amount of modern artillery, including several pom-pom (1lb) and 7lb guns, and a new Creusot 94lb gun (nicknamed 'Big Ben' by the Mafeking defenders), which alone fired 1,497 shells into the town. When Gen. Cronje departed after conducting only six weeks of the siege, his successor, Gen. Snyman, retained the formidable Creusot and six other guns.

Bombarding Mafeking: state artillerymen laying the big Creusot gun, 'Creechy'. (Dr E.J. Yorke Collection)

Col Hore and his adjutant, Capt. Mundell BSAP. (Dr E.J. Yorke Collection)

THE DAYS
BEFORE BATTLE

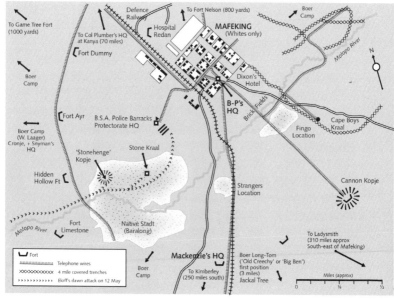

The defence of Mafeking, 1899–1900.

FAMILY MEMORIES OF BADEN-POWELL

Baden-Powell's daughter, The Honourable Betty Clay, recalled an amusing story that her father recounted to her about this momentous meeting with Wolseley at the War Office in London:

Wolseley: Can you sail next Saturday?
B-P: I'm afraid not, sir.
Wolseley: Oh? Why not?
B-P: Because there is no ship sailing that day, but the weekly mail-boat sails Friday, and so I can go then.
(Source: Flower-Smith and Yorke, *Mafeking*, p. xii)

It was in the summer of 1899 that Col Baden-Powell was summoned to a meeting in the War Office by Lord Wolseley, Commander-in-Chief of the British Army, with instructions to lead a small mission of regular army officers to South Africa. Their task, as the 'war clouds' gathered, was to recruit two regiments of irregular mounted troops which, on the outbreak of war, were 'to act as bait for the Boers on the western frontier of the Transvaal and Orange Free State and to divert as many Boer commandos as possible from the main theatre of operations' (Godley, *Life of an Irish Soldier*).

After arriving in Rhodesia in August 1899, and upon successfully raising two regiments of Mounted Infantry, Baden-Powell faced the extremely daunting task of organising the defence of the Rhodesia and Bechuanaland frontiers – a truly vast area of territory. As Baden-Powell himself observed, he was facing acute overstretch:

As war became imminent I saw that my force would be too weak to effect much if scattered along the old border (500 miles), unless it was reinforced with some men and good guns. I reported this, but, as none were available, I decided to concentrate my two columns at Tuli and Mafeking,

THE RAILWAY COMMUNITY

The Railway Contingent at Mafeking was of key tactical and strategic significance. Comprising 132 men, 46 women and 86 children, the workshops housed eighteen locomotives, only one of which was damaged by shellfire, and a large amount of rolling stock valued in total at £120,000. A defence railway 1½ miles long was laid around the north-east front, on which the armoured trains did 'good service'. The workshops were put to good use in the siege with three armoured trucks, walls of steel rails, an iron look-out tower, acetylene searchlight, speaking tubes, electric bells, water towers/containers, medicine chests and stretchers constructed there. Two hundred tons of rails were used for the construction of bomb proofs. Large numbers of the railway workers were also deployed as part of the defence force.
(Source: HMSO, *Mafeking*, p. 178)

respectively, as being the desirable points to hold. (HMSO, *The Boer War*, p. 151)

Mafeking soon emerged, politically and strategically, as the more important of the two for the following reasons. Firstly, it acted as the key outpost for Kimberley, Cape Colony and, equally, for the Protectorate and Rhodesia. It represented a significant threat to the weak flank of the Transvaal. In prestige terms, it was at the centre of the large African districts of the north-west, comprising over 200,000 inhabitants. Logistically, Mafeking represented a major storage depot, holding large food and forage supplies before the siege began. Finally, it was also a major communications centre with important railway and engineering workshops.

Mafeking itself, termed by local Africans as 'the place of stones', was a sprawling town about 1,000yd square, located in open, undulating country alongside the north bank of the Molopo River. Located 8 miles from the Transvaal border, it incorporated a white population of about

The chiefs of the Baralongs, with Wessels in the centre. (Dr E.J. Yorke Collection)

Matatse, the 'Queen Mother' of the Baralongs. (Dr E.J. Yorke Collection)

1,000 and an African *stadt* (village/township) of around 6,000–7,000 inhabitants located ½ mile to the south-west of the main town.

Organisation of the Defence (see map of Mafeking defences)

Baden-Powell opted for an extended defence with numerous fall-back positions and decoys/dummy forts. He set up his headquarters (HQ) in Dixon's Hotel, one of the more prominent buildings in this largely one-storey, brick-built and corrugated iron-roofed railway town. In his own words:

I had disposed my garrison over what some of my Officers considered a rather extended perimeter (about 5 or 6 miles), but everything was arranged for drawing in our horns if necessary. However, in the event we were able to maintain our original position, and even further extend it as it became necessary. (HMSO, *Mafeking*, p. 154)

In tactics partly reminiscent of Gen. Gordon's earlier defence of Khartoum in 1884–85, Baden-Powell carefully defined defence sectors, commanded by selected officers and connected by telephone lines to the various dugouts and forts such as 'Fort Ayr', 'Fort Nelson' and 'Limestone Fort'. Both live and dummy dynamite minefields were sown around the approaches to the town. The railway embankment, located north and south of the Molopo River, provided cover from the east and south-east heights on the southern bank. To the west of the railway and located on both sides of the river lay the African *stadt*. The edge of the *stadt* was entrenched, loopholed and garrisoned by the loyal, mainly Baralong, inhabitants. The ground to the west commanded the *stadt* and represented a potentially vulnerable sector, which was later exploited by the attackers.

The women's laager, Mafeking. (Dr E.J. Yorke Collection)

Sounding the alarm. The mounted orderly is sounding the bugle call which required every man to go to his allotted place. A cyclist orderly beside him awaits orders. Large bells were used for the purpose of warning the townspeople when the Boer artillery began to fire. (Dr E.J. Yorke Collection)

Baden-Powell's official defence force comprised around 700 white Europeans, of whom twenty were imperial army. They comprised the Protectorate Regiment, the British South Africa Police (BSAP), the Bechuanaland Rifles (volunteers) and the Cape Police, who were used to man the forts and outworks. The Cape Police were the local police and the British South Africa Police were based in Rhodesia and already had a base in Mafeking. The Bechuanaland Rifles were almost entirely Mafeking men.

There was also a half-trained element, notably the Railway Contingent, which was raised in a few days from the railway staff and other employees in the town, and the Town Guard, comprising local white militia employed to protect the town itself. Other significant units included the Cape Boy Contingent, raised largely from the Cape black/Fingo groups, and 300 Africans enrolled as cattle guards, watchmen, police etc. One of the key positions, albeit isolated and located over 2,000yd to the south of Mafeking, was an old circular stone fort built by Lt Gen. Sir Charles Warren in 1885 with an interior diameter of around 25yd. The town was

AFRICAN POPULATION OF MAFEKING (BADEN-POWELL'S ESTIMATE):

Baralongs: 5,000
Fingoes, Shangaans and district Baralongs: 2,000
Total: between 7,000 and 8,000
(Source: HMSO, *Mafeking*, p. 177)

Mr Frank Whiteley, Mayor of Mafeking during the siege. (Dr E.J. Yorke Collection)

The Nordernfelt in the extreme outpost trench. (Dr E.J. Yorke Collection)

ARISTOCRATIC DEFENDERS

A significant number of Mafeking's defenders were linked to Britain's elite families. Major the Lord Edward Cecil DSO, Chief Staff Officer to Baden-Powell, was the fourth son of Lord Salisbury, the prime minister. Others included Capt. Lord Charles Cavendish-Bentinck, squadron leader in the Protectorate Regiment, and Capt. The Honourable Charles FitzClarence, Royal Regiment of Fusiliers, who was D Squadron leader in the Protectorate Regiment. Both were later praised for their exceptional courage and leadership, with FitzClarence winning a VC for his gallant sword and bayonet charge into Boer trenches. Others included Capt. the Hon. Douglas Marsham, British South Africa Police (BSAP), son of the Earl Of Romney, who was later killed in the defence of Cannon Kopje, and Lt The Honourable Algernon Hanbury-Tracy of The Royal Horse Guards, who was Baden-Powell's Intelligence Officer. Amongst the civilians was Lady Sarah Wilson, the aunt of Winston Churchill, who emerged as a redoubtable figure in sustaining the morale of the garrison.

well equipped with medical facilities at Victoria Hospital, which comprised five doctors/surgeons and a small team of professional and volunteer nurses, including Nurse Craufurd, who wrote an interesting diary of the siege.

The Shangaans were refugees from the Johannesburg mines and were sent into Mafeking under Boer pressure on the outbreak of war. Many were experienced diggers and they were widely utilised for working gangs on the defences. However, as 'alien' groups lacking local kinship ties, they were to prove extremely vulnerable when food ran short later in the siege. The 'district Baralongs', Fingos and Cape Boys were forced into Mafeking when their villages were burnt and their cattle looted by the Boers. They proved a fertile recruiting ground as armed cattle guards/raiders and as police, watchmen etc. Overall, as we shall see, the African role in defending Mafeking remains significantly underestimated and, in particular, the Baralongs were to play a critical role in winning the defensive action on 25 October 1899 and in the bloody repulse of the final Boer attack of 12 May 1900.

THE BATTLEFIELD:
What Actually Happened?

The Siege of Mafeking can be conveniently divided into three distinct phases. Firstly, the 'Cronje phase', occurring between mid-October and mid-November 1899, after the siege commenced and when the first serious skirmishes and probing attacks took place. Secondly, the 'crisis phase', lasting from December to April when the siege intensified and greatly deteriorated after Baden-Powell's forces had been severely beaten at Game Tree Fort, and when serious food shortages and disease outbreaks became apparent. Finally, the 'relief and recovery phase', which lasted from April to May/June when the 'last gasp' Boer attack by Cmdt Eloff was decisively repulsed, when relief finally arrived on 17 May, and when order and stability in the surrounding districts was gradually restored.

Phase 1: The 'Cronje Phase', 14 October to mid-November 1899: Opening Shots

14 October	Five Mile Bank Skirmish – successful British repulse of probing Boer forces	
25 October	First major Boer assault again defeated by British, with Baralong defenders playing crucial role	
27 October	Successful British night attack against encroaching Boer trenches	

1899

31 October   Failed Boer attack on Cannon Kopje

7 November   Successful British attack on Boer western laager

During the six-week phase of the siege, the Boer commander, Gen. Cronje, made several determined attempts to both infiltrate and overrun Mafeking's defences. As Baden-Powell reported: 'These attacks we beat off [and] of these "kicks", we delivered half a dozen on the 14th, 20th, 25th, 31 October and 7 November' (HMSO, *Mafeking*, pp. 153–4). Each of these successful actions will now be briefly analysed to demonstrate both the resourcefulness and robustness of Mafeking's defenders.

Gen. Cronje and some of the others who besieged Mafeking. (Dr E.J. Yorke Collection)

One of the Boer forts outside Mafeking. (Dr E.J. Yorke Collection)

The First Clash of Arms: Five Mile Bank, 14 October 1899

This first significant action of the siege took place around Five Mile Bank, after British reconnaissance patrols led by Lord Charles Cavendish Bentinck exchanged shots with a strong party of Boers along the railway, 3 miles north of the town. Baden-Powell promptly ordered out the armoured train under Capt. Williams (BSAP) to pressurise the Boers and '… as I wanted to make the first blow felt by them to be a really hard one' (HMSO, *Mafeking*, pp. 186–7). The train was equipped with a 1lb Hotchkiss gun and a .303 Maxim, and accompanied by fifteen BSAP officers.

A squadron of the Protectorate Regiment, led by Capt. FitzClarence, was also despatched in support of the armoured train.

On arrival, Capt. FitzClarence was confronted by a strongly reinforced Boer commando armed with a 7lb Krupp and 1lb Maxim gun, which, after dismounting his men, he proceeded to attack with his left flank protected by the train. He was held up by heavy enemy fire for fifteen minutes, but eventually drove the Boers back and successfully repulsed several attempts to encircle his flank.

Meanwhile, Baden-Powell despatched further British reinforcements comprising of an additional troop led by Lord Charles Bentinck and accompanied by a 7lb gun. The fire from the armoured train and Bentinck now became decisive, forcing the Boer gun out of action before it had fired a shot and driving the enemy Maxim from the field.

The engagement had lasted approximately four hours and, despite being outnumbered, Capt. FitzClarence's courage, discipline and perseverance had more than made up for his manpower deficiency. The British returned to a hero's welcome. Nurse Craufurd recalled: '… soon we heard cheering and ran out and saw our troops coming home after their first fight … we waved to them and cheered them and they looked so tired, but smiled and waved their caps when they saw us. It was sad

The Boers manning their trenches outside Mafeking. (Dr E.J. Yorke Collection)

to see the riderless horses' (Craufurd, p. 61). British losses were a mere two killed, sixteen wounded and one missing compared to fifty-three Boer dead (including four field cornets) and a large, yet still undetermined, number of wounded (*The Times* war correspondent J. Angus Hamilton estimated a figure of 107). In Baden-Powell's view: '… this smartly fought little engagement had a great and lasting moral effect on the enemy' (HMSO, *Mafeking*, p. 188).

The First Major Boer Assault on the Town, 25 October 1899

At noon on 25 October, following a prolonged bombardment from the east and south by seven guns, lasting from 6.30 a.m. till midday, an estimated 3,000-strong Boer force commenced a general advance against the town from the south-west, east and north-east. The Boer main thrust, however, was directed against the African *stadt*. As the Boers commenced rifle fire at extreme ranges of 1,000-2,000yd, the British defenders reserved fire for much closer distances. The Boers soon faced a fusillade of rifle volleys and Maxim machine-gun fire and, perhaps to the surprise of the British garrison, rapidly withdrew from all points. British casualties were confined to one man wounded. Boer losses remained unknown, although Maj. Baillie recalled that British frontal fire, reinforced by enfilading fire from the loyal Baralong shotguns and rifles in the *stadt*, were 'killing many' (Flower-Smith, p. 53). Flower-Smith argues that the reluctance of the Boers to launch a determined frontal attack 'may well have been influenced by Kruger's instructions to limit casualties to not more than 50 killed', and the 'experience of the losses of the skirmish of the 14 October doubtless contributed to Cronje's lack of vigour in pressing this attack' (Flower-Smith, p. 54).

Equally, the Boers were probably shocked by the level of resistance from the African defenders of the *stadt*, which would help explain Cronje's enraged message, delivered to Baden-Powell four days later on 29 October (see quote in Introduction), deprecating the use of armed Africans. Baden-Powell's brave and loyal Baralong had clearly and unexpectedly presented as much a new military threat as a potent challenge to the social order.

Indeed, Baden-Powell reinforced this military ramification, which underlines the vital Baralong role in repelling the first major Boer assault and the generally important role played by the African defenders of Mafeking:

It was afterwards (18 December) ascertained that the attack on the Stadt was intended as a feint while the main attack should come off to northward, on our western face. The Boers had expected the Baralongs not to fire on them, and so advanced more openly than they would otherwise have done.

Their loss was, therefore, pretty heavy, and, surprised at their rebuff, they fell back altogether. (HMSO, *Mafeking*, p. 189)

Capt. Charles FitzClarence VC of the Royal Fusiliers, who showed conspicuous bravery in commanding the Protectorate Regiment during the attack on the armoured train at Mafeking on 14 October, in leading his troops into the enemy's trenches at night about a fortnight later, and particularly in the attack on Game Tree Fort. (Dr E.J. Yorke Collection)

British Surprise Night Attack on the Boer Trench Network, 27 October 1899

Over the next two days the Boers had moved their advanced trenches closer towards the east face of the Mafeking defences, with some constructed as close as 1,200yd. Baden-Powell decided to launch a bayonet attack against the main Boer advanced trench, commanded by Cmdt Louw, in order to deter their further progress. A night attack was therefore organised, with Capt. FitzClarence leading a squadron of his own Protectorate Regiment and a twenty-five man party of Cape Police, led by Lt Murray. Guiding lights were hoisted, by which Capt. FitzClarence was able to lead his party past the flank of the main trench.

The British attacking force moved off at 9.30 p.m. in silence, with magazines charged but no cartridges in the chamber, the

GARRISON FUEL SUPPLY

Coal: 300 tons available at railway store was used for
armoured train, ordnance foundry, pumping station, flour
mills, forage factory and forges etc.
Wood: 25,000lb weekly for bakery, soup and oat-sowen
kitchen, cooking etc. Procured from roofs of huts in the
stadt, old wagons, lopped trees and fencing etc.
Petroleum: Asbestos stove made, but was not a
success.
Patent Fuel: Cow dung and coal dust, mixed in
equal parts and baked, produced 20 tons of
good fuel.
(Source: HMSO, *Mafeking*, p. 173)

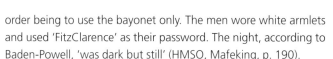

order being to use the bayonet only. The men wore white armlets
and used 'FitzClarence' as their password. The night, according to
Baden-Powell, 'was dark but still' (HMSO, Mafeking, p. 190).

The squadron attained its position on the left rear of the enemy's
trench without being challenged or fired at. Capt. FitzClarence
then wheeled up his men and, with a cheer, charged into the main
and a subsidiary trench, clearing both with the bayonet. Capt.
FitzClarence was himself reputed to have personally killed four of
the Boer enemy with his sword.

The wholly surprised Boer enemy in the rear trenches wildly
opened fire, on occasions against their own fleeing men. The
Cape Police duly returned fire from a flank, in order to both draw
the fire towards themselves and facilitate Capt. FitzClarence's
squadron's safe return. Boer casualties were officially recorded
as forty killed and wounded with the bayonet and sixty killed
and wounded by rifle fire. British casualties were six killed, nine
wounded (including a slightly wounded Capt. FitzClarence) and
two missing (captured by the enemy). A triumphant Baden-
Powell observed: 'The whole operation was carried out exactly
in accordance with instructions and was a complete surprise'
(HMSO, *Mafeking*, p. 189–90).

Boer Attack on Cannon Kopje, 31 October 1899

On 31 October, Gen. Cronje launched a major offensive comprising around 1,000 men against the Cannon Kopje strongpoint, lying to the south of Mafeking. This rocky feature, housing a 20-year-old fort, was of great tactical significance. Around 200ft high and representing one of the few areas of high ground, it occupied a commanding position over Mafeking town. The fort was garrisoned by Col Walford, who was commanding fifty-seven men of the BSAP with two Maxims and one 7lb gun.

The Boer offensive commenced with heavy concentrated shellfire directed against Cannon Kopje from the south-eastern heights, the racecourse to the east and from Jackal Tree to the south-west. Baden-Powell considered that the fire was 'well-aimed', although 'for a time little harm was done beyond knocking down parts of the parapet and smashing the iron supports of the lookout tower', adding 'most of the garrison were lying in the trenches some 80 yards in rear of the fort' (HMSO, *Mafeking*, p. 192). The British gun and the two Maxims were also stowed away for safety during the shellfire, but the telephone wire was cut early in the battle, presumably isolating Baden-Powell's HQ from his tiny garrison.

After thirty minutes of steady and accurate artillery fire, the Boers, who had been massing on the high ground south and south-east of the fort, began to advance in a line of skirmishers from three sides at once. They were supported by other parties and some Boers approached to within 300yd of the fort. Meanwhile, a large Boer force had also deployed in the Molopo Valley, south-east of the town, with the probable intention of storming the town after Cannon Kopje had been captured.

In a move reminiscent of First World War defensive tactics, as the Boer enemy entered within range of the fort, the tiny British garrison moved up from their trench and manned the parapets and Maxims. Here they suffered their first significant casualties from shellfire, but they were now in a consolidated position to repel or deter any frontal assault. Moreover, as the enemy sustained their advance,

Casting shells for 'Lord Nelson'. (Dr E.J. Yorke Collection)

Baden-Powell despatched Capt. Goodyear's Colonial Contingent to occupy a ridge above them and thereby enfilade the Boer's attacking line on the flank. However, they could not be persuaded to move and, as the Maxim at the Ellis's Corner position of Cannon Kopje Fort jammed, the British defence became dangerously stalled.

It was then that Baden-Powell took a decisive initiative by deploying a 7lb gun from under cover of houses near the south-east corner of the town. Directed by Lt Murchison, this opened galling fire on the Boer line as it neared the British fort. Baden-Powell recalled: 'The gun made excellent practice, every shell going in among them and effectively stopped the further advance of the Boers' (HMSO, *Mafeking*, p. 193). As the Boer attack wavered, the reopening of the guns on Cannon Kopje completed the rout.

The British casualties numbered six killed, including Capts Marsham and Pechell, and five wounded. Boer casualties were unknown, but J.A. Hamilton estimated that they lost around forty men. However, Baden-Powell suggested that Boer losses were much greater: 'The enemy's loss was not known, but ambulances were seen about the field picking up for a considerable time, and native spies reported there was much mourning in the laagers,

Capt. Vernon, repeatedly wounded and eventually killed in the attack on Game Tree Fort. (Dr E.J. Yorke Collection)

and that several cart loads of dead had been brought in and buried' (HMSO, *Mafeking*, Maj. Gen. Baden-Powell to Chief Staff Officer (CSO) to Lord Roberts, 18 May 1900).

It was a decisive British victory, clearly demonstrating Baden-Powell's defensive skills, although not without the odd critic. Siege chronicler J.A. Hamilton, for instance, accused Baden-Powell of 'folly' for leaving the fort unprotected with little overhead cover against shells and bullets, and of the profound absence of loopholes for which 'we have paid a heavy price'. Its beneficial impact can, however, be assessed more decisively from a Boer perspective, as they never again risked a frontal attack on this scale until the Eloff attack in early May 1900, over six months later.

The British Surprise Attack on the Boer Western Laager, 7 November 1899

On the back of this success, and in order to forestall a rumoured future Boer attack from their western laager, Baden-Powell decided to launch a daring pre-emptive strike against it as part of his general 'active defence' strategy. At 2.30 a.m. on 7 November,

Maj. Godley duly paraded his force comprising two 7lb guns, one 1lb Hotchkiss (under Maj. Panzera), one dismounted sixty-man squadron (under Capt. Vernon) and one mounted thirty-man troop of the Bechuanaland Rifles (under Capt. Cowan). The opposing Boer force was estimated to number 250 men.

The British troops moved out along the heights to about 1,500yd in advance of Maj. Godley's original position. Capt. Vernon's squadron led in attack order with the guns positioned to his left rear and the Bechuanaland Rifles covering his right rear. At 4.15 a.m. the British guns opened up on the Boer positions at 1,800yd, and the squadron fired volleys, by alternate troops, into the enemy's camp, over which they had full command from the heights they were positioned on. The surprise was complete, with the Boer enemy bolting in all directions to take cover.

The Boer 1lb Maxim and 7lb Krupp in the nearby Beacons Fort soon responded in kind with a heavy and well-directed fire, while large bodies of reinforcements began to emerge from the main Boer south-west laager. Maj. Godley thereupon commenced withdrawing his forces. The British artillery retired first; the Bechuanaland Rifles occupying Fort Ayr to cover the retirement,

The garrison and townspeople in Mafeking showed ingenuity and versatility by making their own gunpowder, their own shells and, in one case, even their own cannon. (Dr E.J. Yorke Collection)

'The Wolf', the little howitzer made in Mafeking. (Dr E.J. Yorke Collection)

'which they did very effectively against a wing of mounted Boers who had worked round to our [the British] right flank' (HMSO, *Mafeking*, p. 195). The Boers brought a very heavy rifle fire to bear on the whole force, but the retirement was carried out 'with the greatest steadiness'. The last stage of the British retirement was covered by the 7lb gun at the west end of the *stadt* and by the Cape Police Maxim and escort. Baden-Powell observed one conspicuous act of bravery in the course of the retirement:

> Our 1lb Hotchkiss upset and broke the limber hook. With their reinforcements, overall Boer strength had reached between 800 or 1,000 men; Gunners R. Cowan and H. Godson very pluckily stood up and repaired damage with rope etc., and got the gun away safely under heavy fire from enemy's 1lb Maxim and 7lb Krupp and rifle fire. (HMSO, *Mafeking*, p. 196)

British losses were minor – five men wounded and five horses killed, with thirty-six cattle in the 'refugee laager' killed and wounded by bullets. Enemy losses remained undetermined, but Baden-Powell noted: 'Three of the enemy's ambulances were seen picking up their casualties after the action, and we afterwards learnt that they had lost a considerable number' (HMSO, *Mafeking*, p. 196). Already, however, food supplies were coming under pressure. Pte Frederick Saunders of the Bechuanaland Rifles recalled: 'In the middle of November the rations were sharply cut ... we were issued with "sowen cards" and were entitled to an issue of a pint a day of this thin milky gruel mixture.' (Saunders, *Mafeking Memories*, p. 180).

Baden-Powell's October and November siege tactics during this first phase of the fighting have attracted criticism from one major source. Thomas Pakenham has observed that his 'raiding parties' were 'expensive in casualties' – about a sixth, 163 of the garrison (ten times the casualty rate at Ladysmith), were killed, wounded or missing during this period – and more scathingly that:

> B-P [Baden-Powell] had survived first two months ... partly owing to his own audacity, partly owing to the good fortune of having Cronje for an enemy. There can be no doubt that if any Boer commander worth his salt had commanded the six thousand besiegers, B-P's men would now have been enjoying a quiet game of cricket in the prisoner-of-war camp in Pretoria. (Pakenham, p. 401)

GARRISON WATER SUPPLY

This was managed by Maj. Vyvyan and Maj. Hepworth. Despite the Boers cutting off the water supply from the waterworks during the first few days of the siege, a sound water supply for the house tanks was sustained throughout the siege. This was largely because the season was unusually wet and the garrison main water source, the Molopo stream, did not run dry. However, contingency plans were undertaken with the cleaning out of various wells and a new one of great capacity was dug.

The water from these was issued to the town and garrison by means of tank wagons, filled nightly and posted at convenient points during the day.

This view can, however, be balanced by citing the scale of the 'bloody nose' Baden-Powell had inflicted on his Boer enemy during this period, as well as re-emphasising his clearly skilful defensive tactics – a judicious mixture of bluff and aggression. Baden-Powell himself conservatively estimated that his forces had inflicted no less than 600 Boer casualties (even the 'enemy' Transvaal newspapers had recorded far more – 287 Boer killed and 800 wounded – which was equally destructive and accounting for up to a sixth of *their* forces!) (HMSO, Baden-Powell to CSO to Lord Roberts, 18 May 1900). It was surely a price worth paying, especially as the probably demoralised Boers, under their admittedly more cautious commander, Gen. Snyman, never attempted another major frontal attack until early May 1900.

Phase 2: Crisis, December 1899–March 1900

1899	5 December	Great storm destroys large areas of British defences
	26 December	Game Tree Fort battle: a major British disaster
1900	9 January	Serious rationing begins in Mafeking
	Late January	First signs of starvation amongst African population of Mafeking
	8 February	Baden-Powell receives telegram from Roberts postponing relief by four months
	19 February	Mafeking authorities establish first soup kitchens for starving Africans
	27–28 February	Baden-Powell's two attempts to evacuate starving 'Transvaal African' groups fail after collapse of truce with Boers
	March	Mafeking African (mainly Baralong) cattle raiding parties score major successes, notably the Madibi raid
	Late March	Acute starvation reported, especially in Transvaal/Shangaani African locations. Numbers of soup kitchens expanded

Serio-comic warfare, after a sketch by Col Baden-Powell. (Dr E.J. Yorke Collection)

On 5 December a visit from 'mother nature' inflicted severe damage on the Mafeking defences far exceeding any losses incurred by earlier Boer attacks. J.A. Hamilton powerfully described the destructive scenes:

> ... shortly before noon, clouds were bunched high up across the sky and over the Boer laager. From where we were in the town it was quite apparent that the temporary centre of the storm was almost above the emplacements of the enemy artillery. Before the breeze had increased the Boers had thrown a few shells into the town, but presently, as the force of the gale struck us, it was evident that the rain-filled clouds were discharging their contents ... the veldt was quickly flooded, the dried up spruits [stream/tributary] were soon charged with foaming cataracts, Mafeking itself lay under water, the earthworks around the town were swept away, trenches and bomb-proof shelters were choked with eddying streams, everywhere was ruin – destruction and complete chaos reigned until the storm had spent itself. (Hamilton, *Siege*, pp. 149–50)

It was a major and totally unexpected setback for the garrison, with parts of it swamped by up to 8ft of water; the only consolation being that the Boer enemy had been equally hard-hit. Hamilton continued:

> As the wind shifted the gloomy masses of vapour we saw through the whirling mist, the Boers, rain-soaked as ourselves, standing disconsolately upon their muddy parapets. They did not seem to understand what they should do … These men, themselves, stood still, shaking the water from their limbs, attempting to dry their weapons. (Hamilton, *Siege*, pp. 149–50)

Worse was still to come on the military front, but at least Christmas provided a brief respite from the growing rigours of the siege. On Christmas Eve, for instance, Lady Wilson held a party for about 250 of the garrison children and, in the evening, she hosted a dinner for Baden-Powell and his staff. Meat supplier Ben Weil provided a turkey and a lavish dinner was laid on in the Mafeking Hotel. Others held parties and dinners in town; the Protectorate Regiment held theirs in Dixon's Hotel. But all the Christmas joy soon evaporated with the horrifying news of the 'Black Boxing Day' disaster at Game Tree Fort.

The Game Tree Fort Disaster, 26 December 1899

The Boer strongpoint at Game Tree Fort, 2,500yd north of the town, had proved to be a continuing problem for the British defenders. The Boers had already heavily bombarded the town from this position and the fort had both 'checked grazing in that direction, and it commanded our line of communication northward' (HMSO, *Mafeking*, pp. 196–7). Baden-Powell decided to attack the position before the Boers further strengthened it and made it impregnable. Unfortunately, the battle proved to be a devastating failure and arguably represented the greatest military blunder of Baden-Powell's hitherto successful military career.

The attack on Game Tree Fort. (Dr E.J. Yorke Collection)

C and D squadrons of the Protectorate Regiment were designated to spearhead the attack from the left flank of the fort, supported by the armoured train the Bechuanaland Rifles and a small twenty-man contingent of the BSAP, while three guns and a Maxim prepared the way from the right flank. The force was commanded by Maj. Godley.

Interior of Game Tree Fort from a photograph taken immediately after the town was relieved. (Dr E.J. Yorke Collection)

Capt. Sandford and his gun from a photograph taken on Christmas Day, the day before the assault on Game Tree Fort. (Dr E.J. Yorke Collection)

Baden-Powell claimed the initial British bombardment by Maj. Panzera's three 7pdr guns, which was designed to 'soften up' the Boer defences, 'made good practice'. However, Flower-Smith regards this statement as 'questionable', citing Baillie's view that the British shells simply 'burst merrily over the fort' and Hamilton's more damning view that the shells 'burst short or beyond Game Tree with no striking effect' (Flower-Smith, p. 60). The damage to the fort was minimal.

It was an ominous development but, nevertheless, the two squadrons advanced in attack formation. On pressing home they were duly exposed to withering fire from Boer riflemen concealed in pits. Capt. Sandford was one of the first to fall and was replaced by Lt Swinburne. Capt. FitzClarence was shot through the thigh and Capt. Vernon, though wounded twice, managed to reach the fort's outside defences with Lt Paton.

Then came the terrible shock that the fort was 'found to be strongly roofed in and so closed as to be impregnable' (HMSO, *Mafeking*, p. 197). In fact, the roof had been reinforced with steel, the entrance sealed and two tiers of loopholes built into the walls. Flower-Smith succinctly describes the final tragic scenes:

> Paton and Captain Vernon were reduced into firing their revolvers into the fort through the loopholes until they were killed. Bugler Morgan tried using his bayonet but he was shot twice in the legs. Others tried using their bayonets too but were shot down, until the force was compelled to retire as Boer reinforcements were spotted riding to the rescue. (Flower-Smith, p. 61)

Sgt Francis of the Bechuanaland Protectorate Regiment provided one of the most detailed accounts of this costly blunder; one of the rare moments when, in the words of Field Marshal Lord Carver, Baden-Powell 'overreached' himself:

> But now I come to the saddest day of the siege, Boxing Day 1899; Xmas night C Squadron under the direction of Major Godley with our two 7 pounders and quick firing machine guns were sent out under cover of darkness to take up positions for an attack at dawn on Game Tree Fort held by the Boers in some force…. 'A' Squadron were also sent to the Northern Forts to support if required and, ordered to do so, of course I went with them. By some error of judgement or misunderstanding the sun was rising before any movement was made or a gun fired; we had been on the alert and standing to arms at 4 am. The first gun, fired about 5.15 which put the Boers thoroughly on

the *qui vive*, our guns did little or no damage. And then we saw C Squadron advancing splendidly in open order against the enemy's position, very few fell in the advance; and at 500 yards they trued to rush the fort at the point of the bayonet. They actually got right up to and fired through the loopholes with rifle and revolver but the place was impregnable. It was about 80 yards square roofed in with iron, sand bags and earth, the walls being quite 9 feet high and only one narrow entrance at the back. It was not to be and orders to retire were given which was carried out and in good order and with no panic but the losses were terrible. Men fell on all sides and the marvel is how any returned alive. When firing ceased and our ambulance wagons went out with an armoured train on the line, the former were soon filled and had to return twice to the scene of the battle; the Dutch crowding round them and robbing the dead and wounded of articles of value and all their weapons. Our losses were 26 killed and 3 taken prisoners. It terribly upset us all and made us all very indignant at somebody else's blunder … the whole Squadron was one recruited from Cape Town and the loss of so many brave men was a serious weakening of our little garrison. (Francis Papers, NAM, 1974-01-138 and Carver, p. 149)

J.A. Hamilton's eyewitness account of the aftermath of the battle was even more poignant:

The heavy vapour from the shells still impregnated the air, and hanging loosely over the veldt were masses of grey-black and brown-yellow smoke clouds. Boers on horseback and on foot were moving quickly in all directions. The scene here was immensely pathetic and everywhere there were dead or dying men … The attitude of the Boers around us was one of stolid composure, not altogether unmixed with sympathy … big and burly, broad in their shoulders, ponderous in their gait, and uncouth in their appearance combining a somewhat soiled and

tattered appearance with an air of Triumph… Here and there they
made some attempt to rob the wounded and despoil the dead.
(Hamilton, pp. 175–6, 182–7, enclosed in Pakenham, p. 405).

Pte Saunders, however, noted one instance of successful British
resistance to Boer trophy collectors: 'An important-looking Boer
walked over to where Captain FitzClarence was lying – he had
been shot through both buttocks – and attempted to take the
Captain's sword. The Captain strenuously objected, refusing
to relinquish the sword, and managed to retain his weapon'
(Saunders, *Mafeking Memories*, p. 96).

The 'despoiling' of the British dead and wounded excited some
vehement protest from the British authorities and not wholly
without success. After Hamilton remonstrated with a Boer officer,
it was reported that Bugler Morgan, who had been robbed of
£3 and his silver watch whilst lying wounded, was reimbursed
with the items by a Boer orderly the next day as he lay in hospital
(Flower-Smith, p. 61).

Victoria Hospital was swamped with casualties, with Nurse
Craufurd recalling the event as 'the saddest during the siege'.

A scene on the battlefield of Game Tree Hill during the truce,
26 December 1900. The Boers on this occasion crowded round the
British wounded with sympathetic interest. (Dr E.J. Yorke Collection)

A 'much depressed' 19-year-old Pte Saunders witnessed the Boer-escorted 'humble farm wagons carrying our dead' back to his sentry position at the cemetery, the bodies:

> surrounded by several weeping women and their children … laid on the bottom of the trench … lying in the same position they died in. No shrouds, no caskets, their faces covered by handkerchiefs … one trooper had died with his hands in front of his face, as though he saw death approaching and tried to ward it off. As the earth was being shovelled, a falling clod struck one of the raised palms. The arm bent back under the impact, then sprang forward, throwing the clod upward, Shovelling was stopped. Troopers jumped into the trench and vainly examined the body for signs of life. That day I lost some of my boyhood. (Saunders, *Mafeking Memories*, pp. 99–100)

The British losses were catastrophic, with three officers and twenty-one NCOs and men dead, and FitzClarence and twenty-two men wounded. Although there were strong suspicions of treachery by the town's Dutch inhabitants, who may have given advance warning of the British attack, Baden-Powell was honest enough to take full blame for the rare blunder: 'If blame for this reverse falls on anyone it should fall on myself, as everybody did their part of the work thoroughly well, and exactly in accordance with the orders I issued' (HMSO, *Mafeking*, pp. 197–8). Flower-Smith, however, opines that the strength of the Boer defences had been clearly miscalculated and 'possibly previous successes had made the garrison over-confident and led them to underestimate their enemy' (Flower-Smith, p. 62).

By January 1900 the situation looked increasingly bleak for the garrison, as African interpreter Sol Plaatje observed:

> Another shell burst in the south … we wonder how long this is going to last. Instead of getting brighter, the prospect in front of us is darkening itself. I am inclined to believe that the Boers

have fully justified their bragging, for we are citizens of a town of subjects of the richest and the strongest empire on earth and the burghers of a small state have successfully besieged us for three months – and we are not even able to tell how far off our relief is. It is certain that it cannot be too near. (Sol T. Plaatje, Mafeking Diary, 3 January 1900)

It was during the months of January, February and March that the full rigours of the siege became apparent to the Mafeking inhabitants. In the wake of the extremely demoralising Game Tree Fort disaster, and the news of the British reverses of 'Black Week' during December 1889, military pressures on the garrison increased. As if to 'rub in' their Christmas victories, Boer gunners celebrated New Year's Day with a vengeance. Mr Algie, the town clerk, counted twenty-one shells fired from 'Old Creechy' that day, together with forty smaller ones and those from a 1lb Maxim gun (Algie Diary, 1 January 1900). At times the shelling could be brutally indiscriminate. Ross noted how, on 3 January, 'nearly all the shells landed in or about the women's laager, one shell bursting in the midst of some little children, killing one and mortally wounding another' (Ross Diary, 3 January 1900). Another morning, as Nurse Craufurd was busy in the hospital, 'washing my patients – shell after shell – 94-pounders – passed overhead. I ran out sometimes to see where they were falling and every one – nine – went into the women's laager' (Craufurd Diary, 1 January 1900). Such indiscriminate shelling caused anger and outrage across the garrison, with Ross calling for 'retribution, short and sharp' (Ross Diary, 1 January 1900).

By 20 January, 'Big Ben' had fired over 800 94lb shells, and such heavy bombardments could result in horrific injuries (Ross Diary, 20 January 1900). On 24 January a 'Big Ben' shell killed one and severely wounded six African women in the *stadt* (Ross Diary, 24 January; see also Algie Diary, 24 January 1900). On 2 January Plaatje reported how another shell from 'Old Sanna' hit the east of the *stadt* and 'amputated an employee [of Ellitson the butcher] in a most piteous manner – both legs and both arms' (Plaatje, Mafeking Diary, 2 January 1900). The flimsy defences of the shelters provided little protection against such a 'monster'. On 1 February a 94lb shell struck one of the splinter-proof sheds at Cannon Kopje 'killing one man [Knox] who was really suffocated before he could be got out, breaking another man's [Francis's] leg and badly wounding another's [T. Goddard] back' (Ross Diary, 1 February 1900). Another 94lb shell 'cut Councillor Dall, Sub Commandant of the Town Council, in half … the first townsman of any standing to be killed since the start of the Siege'. Mrs Dall was left 'prostrate in grief' (Algie Diary, 10 February 1900).

Boer tactics varied considerably, with the artillery guns regularly moved to different firing positions at all times of the day and night. In February new incendiary shells were fired, adding to the terror of the Mafeking inhabitants. Sniper attacks deploying the dreaded long-range Mauser rifle constituted the other most feared tactic by the Boer enemy. Again the shooting could be callous and indiscriminate, with all ages and sexes falling victim to this terror tactic. One poor woman named Poulton was 'shot through the head by a Mauser bullet' as she served her husband's dinner (Ross Diary, 10 January 1900). Some Boer sharpshooters became familiar figures to the garrison. On 15 January it was noted how 'an elderly Boer sniper nicknamed "Old Grey Beard Moses" had been again hard at work with his "ping-bom" [Mauser rifle] ever since daylight this morning' (Ross Diary, 15 January 1900).

The defenders replied with a mixture of tactics – artillery duels, counter-sniping and forays against enemy sniper and gun positions and trenches. Meanwhile, scores of new shells and fuses continued to be ingeniously constructed in the Mafeking homemade arsenal or factory. Much of the sniper activity continued to take place in the Brickfields area, where frontline trenches were barely yards apart and 'territorial rivalry' was high. On 19 January, for instance, Maj. Baillie reported: 'an artillery duel between one of our seven-pounders whose shells were made at our own factory here, and the fuses designed by Lieutenant Daniels, BSAP, in

Maj. Godley's lookout at the western outpost. Maj. Godley sits at the corner of the platform. (Dr E.J. Yorke Collection)

which the shells proved a complete success – the enemy's five-pounder … was almost immediately silenced' (Baillie, 19 January 1900, *Siege*, p. 22). 'Lord Nelson', the ship's gun, continued to shoot with 'great violence' despite its 'doubtful precision' (ibid; see also Ross Diary, 3 January 1900). One successful foray on 1 February, reminiscent of First World War trench tactics, involved Maj. Panzera and Cpl Currie, who 'crept up to the nearest kiln from which the Boers were, unfortunately, absent and had blown it up with 50 pounds of dynamite' (Baillie, 1 February 1900, *Siege*, p. 122). Baillie also recorded a highly successful 300yd sniper duel, which is highly illustrative of the nature of fighting in this 'sniper's paradise' and worth quoting in full:

One Boer who for some extraordinary reason wore a white shirt (which he will never do again) occasionally showed his back over the edge of a shelter he was constructing for himself, acting apparently on the principle of the ostrich. Trooper Piper of the Cape Police eventually got him and at the same moment, his friend, who was firing from the loophole, fired almost simultaneously and got him too, to the huge delight of the Cape Boys. The second man was a bearded man and a well-known sniper – he was an excellent shot and the news of his demise was recorded with unusual pleasure by the garrison. (ibid, probably the same 'veteran' observed by Ross on 15 January)

By the end of February, such steady attritional tactics had resulted in at least one significant military success – Fort Cronje, an important Boer sniper post, was captured, enabling the meagre British artillery to comfortably shell the Boer positions at Game Tree Fort.

For both blacks and whites enduring the Siege of Mafeking, the most serious indication of a growing crisis was the steady onset of stringent food rationing. Already in November, as we have seen, local corn supplies had been commandeered, and Ross observed on 9 January how the authorities were now 'taking over all grocery stocks held by the merchants and townspeople with many things now beginning to run low – no oatmeal, matches, milk, tea etc and … worst of all whisky!' (Ross Diary, 19 January 1900). By 11 January 'all tin stocks' had also been commandeered by the military.

Baden-Powell encountered some entrenched white and black opposition to these measures as penalties for hoarding or price exploitation became progressively stiffer as the weeks passed by. A major target for Baden-Powell was the leading European merchant, Weil, whose demands for a rise of ration prices in early January by 7½p rested on claims of a significant loss of profit. Baden-Powell's view was less than sympathetic: 'I find that by loss he means inability to make the enhanced profit essential to the Siege …

I have declined to raise the price' (Baden-Powell, 4 January 1900, Baden-Powell Papers (BPP)). The most outstanding European example of profiteering was the case of the perhaps aptly named Sgt Maj. Looney, who was arrested by the Commissariat officer, Capt. Ryan, for 'selling stores to townspeople', with one sack of wheat illegally sold by him from government stores accordingly found in a Mr Moore's bedroom! On 18 February, when Looney made a full confession of theft from government stores, Baden-Powell angrily recorded: 'On hearing that I intended to have him shot' (Baden-Powell, Staff Diary, 12 and 18 February 1900, BPP). Instead, on 20 February, Looney was sentenced to be reduced to the ranks and five years' penal servitude, as well as discharged with ignominy, pending an appeal to the commander-in-chief. Plaatje recorded the tense situation in the courtroom and the subsequent public humiliation of this officer:

> Major Godley was presiding, and all the others present were dressed in their best uniforms. The Court was crowded and I left it still in progress … Looney was arraigned on the market square and sentence was promulgated by Major Godley. According to the newspaper on Tuesday, we were allowed to be present at the promulgation. He was sentenced to be reduced from the ranks of His Majesty's Service and to serve five years penal servitude … he was handed over to the civil powers. I felt so sorry for him – such a pretty young fellow. I understand that he has a wife and child. (Plaatje, Mafeking Diary, 5 January 1900, p. 80)

Penalties for African offenders were also harsh. One Alfred Ngidi, already dismissed for being asleep whilst on sentry duty, 'came in for a very rough time. He appeared again this morning on a charge of failing to hand over a bag of Kaffircorn. The sentence of the Court: seven days' hard labour and the confiscation of the Kaffircorn. Hard luck on poor little Alfred' (ibid, 6 January 1900, p. 79). African elite groups were also by no means exempt. Next day, 6 January, a dozen or so of the local people, including the

The Court of Summary Jurisdiction in Mafeking at which a native was tried before Lord Edward Cecil (with black band on arm) for stealing a goat. In this case the thief was sentenced to death. (Dr E.J. Yorke Collection)

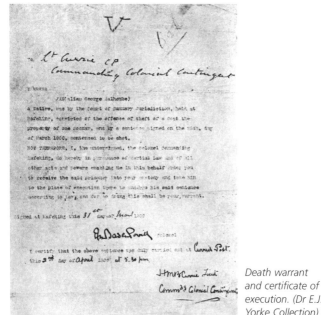

Death warrant and certificate of execution. (Dr E.J. Yorke Collection)

prominent Lumata and Mfazi (Baralong) families, were arraigned 'to answer to a charge of having wrongfully, unlawfully and maliciously neglected to handover their grain when requested by the authorities to do so'. As Plaatje noted: 'Things are getting very serious' (ibid, p. 82).

Specific grain stores were set up by Capt. Ryan, the ever-vigilant Commissariat officer 'where each native was given a number on a metal badge' to ensure that they 'buy a ration at one particular store'. The military authorities, however, remained unnecessarily suspicious of the ways in which Africans disposed of their rations, complaining that 'if we issue Kaffircorn we find the natives at once make a beer and sell it'. However, it was a suspicion based on their ignorance of the African diet. As Plaatje noted, it was a misunderstood viewpoint: 'It came to their notice that some Baralongali [sic] were selling Kaffir beer the other day. They look upon it as wasting … they do not know that Kaffir beer to a common Barolong is "meat, vegetables and tea" rolled into one, and they can subsist entirely on it for a long time' (Plaatje, Mafeking Diary, 5 January 1900, p. 80). Baden-Powell himself soon became aware of African unease over these somewhat harsh policies: 'Baralong natives in the Stadt are getting a little suspicious of us. They want to know … why we are trying to take all their grain from them' (Baden-Powell, 7 January 1900, Staff Diary, BPP). As January progressed, other European and Asian small traders became the particular targets of 'food raids' as 'a good deal of meal etc was being kept undeclared by small traders and … unauthorised bread was being baked and sold illegally'. On one night raid a whole wagon-load of mealies was discovered, hidden away by Indian traders, with the goods being confiscated and the owners duly tried by the Court of Summary Jurisdiction (ibid, 6 January 1900).

As military and social conditions deteriorated in this way, Baden-Powell was forced to exercise even tighter political control over the garrison. Baden-Powell became particularly suspicious of the alleged nefarious activities of members of the Dutch community within the garrison population; these groups, and also individual Africans accused of spying for the Boers, faced harsh penalties. It was noticed how Dutch women and children 'never moved out of their trenches' during the shelling, which suggested that they were well informed by outside intelligence of forthcoming attacks.

The design for this note was made by Col Baden-Powell. 'The Wolf' was the African name for the colonel. (Dr E.J. Yorke Collection)

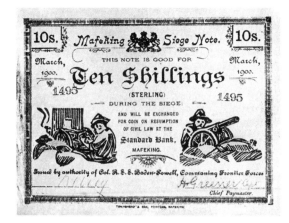

The figures, supposed to represent a Boer and a Briton, are rough reproductions of drawings by Col Baden-Powell. (Dr E.J. Yorke Collection)

Examining horse meat intended for rations. (Dr E.J. Yorke Collection)

Dutch women in the women's laager were also suspected of communicating intelligence to their outside Boer kinsmen about the garrison's defences. On 27 January Ross noted how 'the spy business has now got BP's back properly up … moving all the Dutch women and children and some men out of the jail so that if the enemy do again attempt to shell our women they will kill their own friends' (Ross Diary, 27 January 1900).

Three alleged African 'spies' were eventually executed during the duration of the siege after trial by the Court of Summary Jurisdiction. Thus, on 28 January Ross recorded in his diary: 'Native spy shot today by the Cape Boys at a distance of ten paces. Three bullets going through his head and three through the chest, the force of which drove him backwards instead of falling forwards into the grave' (Ross Diary, 28 January 1900). On 25 January, Baillie recorded full details of this same case of 'a native convicted as a spy … he had been sent in to obtain full information as to the stores, forts, their garrisons, and the general disposition of the forces of the town. He quite acknowledged the justice of his sentence, but only seems to think that is was hard lines that he should be executed before he had time to procure any information at all' (Baillie, 25 January 1900, *Siege*, p. 110).

During this period, censorship of the press was also significantly tightened and Baden-Powell took stern measures against both black and white citizens for seditious or treasonable talk. One interesting case was the arrest of the popular townsman, J.W. de Kock, for 'working against imperial interests'. This measure was seen as excessive, especially as the citizen himself was known for his loyalty. The men of his fort even produced a petition to seek his release on bail. Ross, a close friend of de Kock, was incensed by this example of the growing, unchecked powers of the authorities: 'What a power these autocrats have. They do just as they please in every matter, great and small, even to the liberty of the subject, without

The Mafeking mint. Mr Ross manufacturing £1 notes. (Dr E.J. Yorke Collection)

Where Mafeking did its banking business. (Dr E.J. Yorke Collection)

having to give the slightest reason why or wherefore.' He ominously noted: 'The imperial authorities must take care they do not raise a hornet's nest about their ears' (Ross Diary, 1 February 1900). Under such pressures there were also, on occasions, mutinous mutterings within the garrison's military contingents. Thus, on 1 February, the BSAP men in one fort complained at 'not being treated fairly by being left up there all the time of the Siege and that they should be relieved and changed to different positions'. More serious was the rising rate of desertion. On 25 February, for instance, Baden-Powell angrily noted 'two deserters – out for a ride – never returned – Boer and German' (Baden-Powell, 25 February 1900, Staff Diary).

To control the majority black population within the garrison, Baden-Powell took pains to sustain a typical and elaborate pyramidic hierarchy of social control. As in other colonial societies, a network of black collaborators was sustained and rewarded with payments in cash and kind. At the top of the political hierarchy were the chiefs and leading councillors of the Baralong, all of whom received generous allowances or 'salaries'. The chiefs played a vital role in grain requisition. Thus, Plaatje noted how grain from the *stadt* was 'always carried away by the chiefs... The officers are under the impression that when the chiefs reach a hut they take away the last crumbs they find in possession of the owner who would henceforth survive on what they purchase economically' (Plaatje, 5 February 1900, Mafeking Diary, p. 80). When these African elites proved unreliable or troublesome, they were swiftly replaced. The most notable event in this respect was the deposing of the Baralong paramount chief, Wessels, and his replacement by the leading councillor, Lekoko, in January 1900. This major event in terms of Baden-Powell's political control and manipulation of the indigenous black population has been glossed over by most of the diarists who generally refer to the reasons for his dismissal as 'drunkenness' or 'serious incompetence'. Hamilton, however, provides both a striking account of these proceedings, a politically tense moment in which Baden-Powell firmly stamped his authority on the local African elite, and revealed the real (political) reason for Wessels' deposition. Wessels had, in fact, directly defied the authorities by 'instigating his tribe to refuse to work for the military authorities here, and through his instrumentality [it had] become difficult to obtain native labour and native runners'. He had preached sedition, 'telling them that the English wished to make slaves of them and that they would not be paid for any services they rendered; nor would they ... be given any food but left to starve when the critical moment came' (Hamilton, *Siege*, p. 196).

Hamilton noted how this was an 'interesting meeting ... one which recalled the early days of Africa when the authority of the Great White Queen was not a power paramount in the council chamber of the tribes'. There was some significant resistance. Hamilton observed how, at the news of his supersession, 'the old chief snorted with disgust and endeavoured to coerce his people to reject the demands made upon them, while the majority of the "Khotla" [African Council] attending the "indaba" [meeting] sided with the imperial authorities represented by the Civil Commissioner, Mr Bell'. Hamilton also noted how the 'younger and more turbulent ... spoke at once in any angry chatter and were inclined to express sympathy' (ibid, pp. 197–8. For interesting parallels of large-scale African resistance to colonial war demands later, in the First World War, see Yorke, *Forgotten Colonial Crisis*). In the event, this significant confrontation between the local imperial authorities and this key African elite was safely executed with Wessels significantly placated by the promise of a continuation of his allowance. He was, however, to remain a significant black critic of imperial policies during the remainder of the siege.

Equally, if not more important, were the armed black military, who, as we have seen, played a crucial role in the Brickfields fighting. Mr Algie noted the four groups of 'armed native defenders' who constituted a privileged African class enjoying superior rations and equal pay with their European counterparts. These included the sixty-strong Cape Boys 'made up of the coloured or half-breed servants, storekeepers and gardeners living and working in the town; Fingos, under Mr Webster; a detachment of Baralongs under Sergeant Abrahams and the 'Black Watch' a composite group including a number of Fingo and Zulu tribesmen controlled by Lieutenant Mackenzie (a European)' (Algie Diary, 23 January 1900). All were to play an increasingly significant role, especially during the ensuing three months of the siege. The issue of deploying armed blacks remained a controversial subject and continued to be the focus of angry correspondence between the Boer authorities, who were acutely aware of the implications for white rule and social order in general if this practice became too widespread. In January and February, Snyman again accused Baden-Powell 'of arming and employing natives against us', to which Baden-Powell again replied denouncing such hypocrisy and noting again how Snyman was already deploying 'an armed native watch solely for the purpose of catching our natives who are sent to steal cattle' (Baden-Powell, 21 and 22 January 1900, Staff Diary, BPP). The dangers of wider multi-racial conflict emerged at another 'indaba' with the newly appointed chief, Lekoko, who over-demonstrated his loyalty to his new master by proposing more active armed black participation in the conflict and requesting 'more rifles and ammunition and permission to strengthen his outworks' (Baden-Powell, Lekoko and Council indaba, 22 January 1900, ibid). It was a request swiftly but firmly refused by an alarmed Baden-Powell.

Another significant, albeit unarmed, African collaborative group were the 'trench diggers'. During January, night parties of between 300 and 400 African trench diggers, including already skilled refugee mineworkers from the Transvaal trapped within the garrison, completed a veritable maze of trenches around the besieged town. On 11 January, for instance, Ross noted the 'stupendous' work on the trenches: 'Of course the authorities have paid them for work done but where on earth should we have been without the assistance of their manual labour … It is a great credit to their loyalty and should be recognised by the imperial authorities' (Ross Diary, 11 January 1900). Again, in organising and recruiting trench workers, the newly appointed tribal elite led by Lekoko played a key role, as Ross commented: '… no more loyal and deserving men could possibly be found than Lekoko or Silas Molema, the acting Chiefs of the Baralong nation' (ibid).

Another group perceived as vital to the survival of the garrison were the African runners, scouts and messengers. Under enormous pressures they daily brought in vital intelligence news reports and messages from the approaching relief force and neighbouring besieged garrisons. These tasks were often carried out at the cost of their own lives, if not gross maltreatment when captured by the Boers, with 'punishments' ranging from flogging to mutilation. Thus, on 7 January Baden-Powell cryptically recorded in his staff diary: 'Our runners sent out north and south last night failed to get through Boer outposts' (Baden-Powell, 7 January 1900, Staff Diary, BPP). On 29 January, Ross reported on what came to be a routine tragedy as one African despatch carrier was 'shot by Boers' and also a 'native, her breast cut off for the same offence'. For he and others, these Boer atrocities confirmed 'what ghouls and murderers these great unwashed hogs are!' (Ross Diary, 29 January 1900).

From the logistical perspective, an increasingly important African group were the 'nocturnal' and mainly Baralong cattle raiders who plundered Boer herds and farms outside the perimeter of the garrison. In the words of Hamilton: 'If sniping be the rule by day, cattle raiding by night gives to the natives some profitable employment' (Hamilton, *Siege*, p. 200). On 17 January, for instance, Ross paid tribute to the 'Mafeking Baralongs' who were 'doing more very useful work … having brought in … 18 head, and then another of 22'. He confirmed that 'it would take a very long time to starve at this rate' (Ross Diary, 17 January 1900). Their food supplies were becoming vital. Thus, Baden-Powell had recorded the satisfaction in early January how 'two natives brought in 40 sheep' and later on, on the 15th, he confirmed with delight how 'our native scouts brought in 18 head of fat cattle looted from the Boers' (Baden-Powell, 1 and 15 January 1900, Staff Diary, BPP). Hamilton went even further in his praise, considering such Baralong raids of 'unique value in the garrison … the rich capture which these natives have made has given us a welcome change from bone and skin to juicy beef' (Hamilton, *Siege*, p. 200). As we shall see, even greater successes were to be achieved during the closing months of the siege, with the raiders themselves benefiting from a proportionate system of bounties and rewards of stolen cattle that, undoubtedly, were to help stave off the worst effects of the later food shortages.

For Baden-Powell, it was essentially a 'carrot and stick' system of political control. When not preoccupied, as he often was, with securing the defences of the garrison, he continued to devote considerable time to morale building. After the Game Tree debacle, and with news of British military reverses during 'Black Week', Baden-Powell took great pains to raise the spirits of the garrison. It was a task for which the extrovert Baden-Powell, with his renowned gifts for amateur dramatics, was exceptionally well suited. As before Christmas, a huge variety of entertainment was organised, mainly at weekends, to raise the overall morale of the garrison. On Sunday 21 January, for instance, an 'Agriculture and Produce Show' was organised, including 'stalls displaying vegetables, fruit sewing work and knick-knacks made from shells, bullets, etc. A particular highlight of the show was the prize awarded for the 'best Siege baby' (Algie Diary, 21 January 1900). Mr Algie recorded a typical, if literally more 'action-packed', entertainment weekend organised on 11–12 February, in which Baden-Powell played his usual prominent role:

> The Cycle Sports were cancelled on account of the rain the day before … a cricket match was played between the FitzClarence squad and the Town XI. In the evening the Beleaguered Bachelors' Ball was held but the evening was interrupted by rifle fire. Men were called to their posts although the band played on till midnight. Baden-Powell gave two turns as 'Senor Paderewski' and as 'Gentleman Joe'. (Ibid, 11 February 1900)

The European women in the garrison played a crucial role in these events. Lady Wilson recorded: 'many Union Jacks to be made – a most intricate and tiresome occupation' and these were distributed 'among the various forts' (Wilson, *Memories*, p. 202). The military and civilian diarists of the siege paid fulsome tributes to the value of these events that, in Baillie's words, 'go far to relieve our spleen and vary the interminable monotony of the Siege' (Baillie, 31 January 1900, p. 119). The tension could be relieved in other ways. The garrison was both heartened by, and marvelled at, the frequent displays of sangfroid in the face of the many near misses that occurred amidst the incessant rain of enemy shells and bullets. One noted how Maj. Panzera 'takes the biscuit for coolness' when a shell struck the ground immediately behind him as 'he was walking across the square. All he did was to slew around … swing his fly whisk at the spot' and 'walk on quite unconcernedly' (Ross Diary, 20 January 1900). Another miraculous escape occurred as a massive Boer shell passed through the rooms of the Town Hall, narrowly missing several groups of men (Mafeking volunteers) playing cards in groups (ibid, 19 January

1900). The siege ladies demonstrated similar stoicism, with Lady Wilson experiencing the 'narrowest escape … that it is possible to imagine', as a shell struck a room in the Convent within 'four feet from where we were sitting' (Wilson, *Memories*, pp. 183–4).

Nevertheless, such morale-building events could not disguise the embryonic signs of starvation within the African population. Despite rationing, by the end of January the situation had worsened, as Ross recorded:

> I am very sorry to say the natives in the Stadt are having a very hard time of it. Scarcity of food amongst them, coupled with dysentery and other diseases … is carrying off large numbers. They even now come with their sixpences and tickeys (a colloquial term for the South African three pence coin) all over the town trying to buy peaches, however green they may be on purpose to get a square feed. This alone, I think is sufficient to feed to the microbe of dysentery almost to the extent of it becoming a pestilence. (Ross Diary, 31 January 1900)

Plaatje was already noting the potential for distress amongst the more recently arrived homeless and vulnerable 'miscellaneous collections of natives from Jo'burg [Johannesburg] who thought that the war would last a month or less. They came here as they thought Mafeking was safe enough to spend the month, after which they would return to the revolutionary Rand. They … include Pondos, Shangaans, Barotse, Zambesians and South Central African breeds'. They were:

> … a harmless lot of people – some of them live under the two trees in the space between the BSA Police Camp and the stadt. They do a night's toil when they require a little cash to buy grain that they 'nona' with horse flesh. They are quiet and are waiting for the end of this trouble and I am sure they would not do any harm to anybody. (Plaatje, 3 January 1900, *Siege of Mafeking*, p. 76)

As rationing for both blacks and whites tightened in February, several diarists noted further signs of deterioration amongst some African groups. After bread was reduced to 6oz per man per day, with women receiving 3oz and children 1½oz, Ross noted how the Africans were already 'beginning to look a bit dicky on their half a pound of meal per day' (Ross Diary, 9 February 1900). On 6 February a further key indicator of the beginnings of acute starvation occurred in the town when a horse was killed by one of the Boer 94lb shells: 'The moment the horse was dead the carcass was set upon by a horde of natives, like a lot of Aasvogels [vultures], pulled and cut off the meat and carted it away until there was not a scrap to be seen. Some of them have had a good meal today at any rate' (ibid, 6 February 1900). The horse's name was 'Whiskey' and, in fact, belonged to the court interpreter, Plaatje, who registered his shock at witnessing the terrible fate of his beloved horse at the mercy of this ravenous crowd: 'When I got there I saw only his blood and nothing more of him and a good thing too. A lot of Basutos congregated on the spot and hardly gave him time to die – so much in a hurry were they of getting his meat' (Plaatje, 6 February 1900, *Siege*, p. 93). By 10 February military eyewitnesses also confirmed the potentially dark disaster now looming. Maj. Baillie thus observed: 'The question of food supplies for the native had become very serious.' Presumably, with the continuing success of cattle raids, 'it was not the question of meat so much as the question of grain' (Baillie, 10 February, p. 133). Ada Cock also noted a burgeoning food crisis, as African children 'come here begging for food. Their legs are like sticks and their knees like the door knob and one has nothing to give them' (Midgley, *Petticoat in Mafeking*, p. 68).

On 19 February the authorities took major steps to deal with the mounting food crisis as 'a soup kitchen was opened for natives for the first time' and '800 rations of soup were served out' (Algie Diary, 19 February 1900). Such was the success that 'several other soup kitchens were to be opened in different sections of the town'. Horseflesh soup came as standard issue to the queues of starving Africans, a diet not conducive to all tastes, especially the Fingos. Mr Algie noted how 'Stadt natives jibbed at eating horse soup claiming it caused swollen heads and limbs that resulted in death' (ibid, 27 February 1900). Critics have attacked Baden-Powell for providing such unsavoury and unsuitable rations to the African population. In fact, by the end of February, Baden-Powell, no doubt aware (as Hamilton confirms) that Europeans were also by now being forced to eat this 'damned and disagreeable dish', gave orders for nothing to be issued in lieu to ensure that the Africans 'would be glad to eat it soon' (Hamilton, *Siege*, p. 226; Baden-Powell, 27 February 1900, Staff Diary, BPP).

Earlier, on 8 February 1900, Baden-Powell had received a 'bombshell' telegram from Kitchener that forced him to undertake even more drastic measures. In a paragraph he was ordered to 'make supplies last four months' and 'to send as many women, children and natives as possible away should opportunity offer' (Mafeking Day Book (CSO), Kitchener to Powell, 21 January 1900 incl. in T. Jeal, *Baden-Powell*, pp. 265 and 619).

Recent writers have highlighted logistical blunders by both Kitchener and Roberts, which may account for these severe delays in getting relief to the Mafeking garrison in early 1900. Col Ian Bennett has graphically exposed the 'chaos caused by the transport reorganisation imposed by Roberts and Kitchener in the midst of the war, neither of whom had in depth knowledge of the organisation and administration of the British Army'. They split up and prematurely expanded existing tried and tested ASC regimental – designated supply units, with many newly appointed officers of new units lacking any experience of transport or animal management. The result was anarchy, with large amounts of supplies either lost to or captured by the enemy or unable to reach their designated destinations (see Bennett, *Supply and Transport in the Boer War*, SOQ, pp. 2–10).

Whatever the reasons, the news came as a terrible blow as Baden-Powell's meticulous rationing plans had anticipated the arrival of relief forces over a much shorter time span. He now proposed 'to try to get all natives and foreign natives to leave this place by laying down stocks [of food] through Colonel Plumer at Kanya and stopping the sale in town' (Baden-Powell, 8 February 1900, Staff Diary). It was a controversial decision that has been lambasted by recent critics such as Thomas Pakenham as a ruthless policy of 'leave or starve' (see Pakenham, *Boer War*, pp. 407–9). For Baden-Powell it was clearly a decision based on extreme military imperatives. In fact, he took the trouble to inform and justify his policy to the local Baralong elite, telling them 'that we were to hang on for four months and that though the food would suffice for whites and Baralongs, it would not be enough for the other outside natives as well' – the latter 'must therefore be told to escape as soon as possible and make their way to Kanya' (Baden-Powell, 10 February 1900, Staff Diary, BPP). It represented a terrible dilemma, but, in its defence, Baden-Powell was already acutely aware of starvation deaths in the *stadt* (by 23 February he himself had recorded at least three dead). Moreover, during February there had been successful breakouts by various groups of escapees, which may have given him confidence to try out this policy. For instance, on 22 February thirty Africans had 'got away after dark towards Kanya', and on the 25th 'about half of sixty natives got through Boer lines' (ibid, 22 and 25 February 1900, Staff Diary, BPP). Thirdly, in rationalising this policy of enforced exodus (finally decided on 27 February), Baden-Powell not only provided rations and an armed escort for the departing Africans, but also, perhaps rather naïvely, reached an agreement with the local Boer authorities to allow safe passage. A sympathetic Plaatje thus recorded the preparations made for departure with the arrival of a 'waggon-load of mule flesh' delivered as rations for the journey out. His account confirmed the extreme state of starvation then existing amongst the 'foreign' or Transvaal African groups:

I saw horse flesh for the first time being treated as human food stuff ... it looked like meat with nothing unusual about it but when they went to the slaughter pole for the third time and found there was no meat left and brought the heads and feet, I was moved to see the long ears and bald heads … the recipients, however, were all very pleased to get these heads and they ate them nearly raw. (Plaatje, Mafeking Diary, 27 February 1900, p. 108)

In the event, the evacuation proved to be a disastrous failure from the start as the full escort failed to turn up and the Boers opened fire. Plaatje records the resultant tragic scenes:

When a start was made from the river there arose cries of 'Mma, Mma' [sic], children starting after their mothers and women after their children in the dark; but, after passing the BSA camp beside the heavy treads of twice 900 feet, there reigned a dead silence … the volunteers failed to turn up and 12 men being unable to very well fight and drive 900 people at the same time the Boers scattered the whole crowd in every direction' (ibid, p. 109)

As Baden-Powell confirmed, the 'two or three shots' fired by Boer snipers had caused 'widespread panic' and a subsequent second attempt, after Baden-Powell had re-negotiated a truce, ended in failure as the Boers reneged on their guarantee 'to the effect that they would let native women and children go away – provided they went by day' (Baden-Powell, 27 and 28 February 1900, Staff Diary, BPP). This second *daytime* exodus near Game Tree was thus decimated as the Boers 'opened a fearful fire' amounting, in the view of Ross, to 'nothing else but cold-blooded murder' (Ross Diary, 1 March 1900). A deeply chastened Baden-Powell and the shocked garrison authorities were thus forced to send out doctors 'to render what assistance they could' (ibid).

It was a tragic end to this particular phase of the siege, with this disaster at the end of February being matched by the growing evidence of disease (a potential dysentery and typhoid epidemic) as well as widespread malnutrition amongst the children of the garrison. This included recorded outbreaks of 'Brandsick' or scabs (Cock, 14 February 1900; Midgley, *Petticoat in Mafeking*, p. 66). For the beleaguered garrison, however, much worse was to follow during the remaining three months of the siege:

> The garrison is famished, that is, in reality, the kernel of our situation. Our energies are exhausted because our vital processes are insufficiently nurtured. We are all listless; we feel that the siege has been a strain of the most severe description and we are holding ourselves in for the final rally ... determined to hold the town and occupy, till the end, our posts. (Hamilton, *Siege of Mafeking*, 30 April 1900)

January and February had been an extremely traumatic time for the hard-pressed inhabitants of Mafeking, but, in many respects, the following two months would emerge as the critical period of the siege. As the Boers sustained a relentless military pressure (Mr Algie recording one barrage by 'Old Creechy' of thirty-four shells on Saturday 3 March (Algie Diary, 3 March1900)), the garrison produced more innovations to confound the enemy. The most significant of these was the invention of 'dynamite bombs', a crude form of grenade ostensibly invented by Lt Feltham of the Protectorate Regiment and 'made from jam tins and ... very handy for throwing'. On Sunday 4 March these crude rather eccentric devices scored a notable military success in the Brickfields as Feltham, deploying these grenades both by hand and even by fishing rod, proved 'instrumental in ensuring the success of Captain FitzClarence and Captain Williams' reoccupation of a trench in the Brickfields' (ibid, 4 March 1900). The new homemade garrison gun, the 'Wolf', was also tried out on the east trench, firing about seven shells at 1,000yd at the Boers. However, by the end of March the somewhat overused breech had blown out. According to Ross the following, rather amusing, conversation took place:

BP [Baden-Powell] (On the telephone) to Panzera at the Brickfields: Can the wolf reach their big gun?

Panzera: I think so, by putting in an extra charge of powder, but I am afraid the breech will not stand it.

BP: Try.

Panzera (later): Have fired the gun and the breech has burst.

BP: Damn!

(Ross Diary, 26 March 1900)

The Boers responded by deploying new homemade shrapnel shells, which caused increasing casualties amongst both people and livestock within the garrison precincts. Another new military innovation deployed by the Boer attackers was wire-operated 250lb nitro-glycerine and dynamite mines, which were left behind in vacated trenches in a vain bid to catch the garrison defenders unaware. Fortunately most of these were successfully defused (Baillie, 13 March 1900, *Siege*, p. 175). The killing methods became more barbaric in other ways. Pte Saunders observed: 'Some of the enemy were firing explosive bullets. These exploded on contact. In reply we filed off the nose of bullets, exposing the lead core and filing a cross on the tip, making dum dum bullets. Headquarters got to know about this and posted orders forbidding their use' (Saunders, *Mafeking Memories*, p. 108). On the British side, by early March most of the extensive trench network had been completed, with trenches often acquiring variations of London street names such as Regent's Circus and Oxford Street, while the main Boer trench on the Brickfields 40yd away was appropriately nicknamed 'Hounds Ditch'.

During the two main Brickfields attacks launched during this period, fighting could be ferocious and often hand-to-hand encounters produced numerous examples of both black and white valour, including 'coloured' Sgt Maj. Taylor who was injured and fatally wounded by two successive shell bursts. At times, however, the fighting degenerated into farce with, for instance, the rival

CRIME AND PUNISHMENT IN MAFEKING

Baden-Powell's official record of cases dealt with
by the Court of Summary Jurisdiction:

Charges
House-breaking: 14
Treason: 35
Theft: 197
Minor Offences: 184
Total: 430

Punishments
Death: 5
Corporal Punishment: 115
Detention in gaol: 23
Fines: 57
Imprisonment with hard labour: 91
Total: 291

(Source: Baden-Powell to CSO
Lord Roberts, 18 May 1900,
enclosed in HMSO, *Mafeking*, p. 185)

British and Boer sides in the Brickfield trenches 'throwing stones at each other'; an incident repeated on 10 March when both sides also discarded their rifles (Algie Diary, 9 and 10 March 1900). Truces, increasingly rare and usually held on Sundays, preserved the remnants of a 'gentlemen's war' with friendly exchanges of newspapers and rations, but even these were often violated if either side were seen to be making war-like preparations on this ostensibly 'holy day'.

On the 'home front' behind the garrison defences there was an increasingly rapid deterioration in the standard of life for most citizens. Rationing tightened considerably and, by early April, orders had reduced bread rations from 8oz to 6oz with increasing restrictions on the sale of green mealies and cattle. Bread, a staple part of the garrison diet, had now become a luxury item. For European and African alike, the crude substitute (designed to replace the lost 2oz of bread ration) was a bitter porridge made from oats called 'sowen'. Made by soaking forage oats in water for a long time, skimming off the husks and scum (which could be used for feeding fowls) and then boiling up the remainder with added salt, it was, perhaps, appropriately described by Baden-Powell as 'like paste used for bill-boards' (Algie Diary, 29 March 1900).

During these two critical months, however, both European and African sources again highlight the valuable and increasingly critical role played by the indigenous armed black contingents. Just as the Game Tree Fort battle of December 1899 had produced many white heroes, so the great cattle raids and forays into Boer lines of March and April 1900 produced a significant crop of black heroes. Most singled out for praise were the Baralong cattle raiders. On 3 March, for instance, Ross recalled a great deception of the enemy with two Baralongs who 'engaged themselves as servants to the Boers craftily returning at night with 43 fine head of Boer oxen' (Ross Diary, 3 March 1900). At times the Baralong raiding parties successfully engaged their hated Boer enemies in open battle. Most notable of these skirmishes was the Madibi ambush of 13 March when an eighteen-strong Baralong raiding party, led by the much-fêted Sgt Abrahams, having observed Boers following on the spoor, had doubled back on their own trail and ambushed them at short range. A most impressed Ross recorded their report, a rare first-hand and colourful African account of one of the most successful actions of the siege, and one which revealed the full extent of guile, resourcefulness and sheer raw courage of Baden-Powell's black auxiliaries:

Twenty five of us went out ... when we got to Madibi about 14 miles out we found the Boers were following our spoor so we hid on top of a Kopje. The Boers saw us from the flat and fired at us at long range. When they came a little closer we fired and we saw we had hit one of the men who had stripes on his arm. The Boers went away ... so we left this place and went down to the railway lines at Madibi and got into the gravel pits (formerly used as ballast holes). By and by the Boers again came up following our spoor … we waited until they came up quite close and then fired a volley at them killing eight and wounding seven and killing three or four of their horses. We brought in the arms and horses of the two we killed…. Others are dead but we could not get their things as the Boers took them away. After our volley the Boers galloped away. (Ross Diary, 14 March 1900)

For the Mafeking African community this was seen as a great victory over their hated Boer oppressors. Plaatje testified to the ferocity of this brutal clash of arms between the two antagonistic foes, in which no quarter was given, with one Baralong 'hitting him [a Boer] on the ground and he wounding one of our chaps on the buttocks before another hit him on the forehead'. It was 'a brief but very hot battle'. Plaatje gleefully recorded the booty which included horses ('a beautiful grey gelding') and 'two rifles … a splendid pair of Martinis made especially for the ZAR by Wesley Richards' and 'stamped very neatly "JJ Jonck, ZAR 1900" with a circle' (Plaatje, Mafeking Diary, p. 117). African casualties amounted to only two wounded (one slightly) and their Boer enemy suffering eight dead.

These successes had a massive effect as the Baralong raiders rapidly expanded their activities. A 'white man's war' was rapidly becoming a mixed race war. Plaatje reported on 19 March, for instance, that up to 1,000 armed Baralongs were now 'scattered all over the country. Two hundred of them are at Madibi and they have two Maxims. Mathakgong's [a notorious raider] name is a household name on every farm … they say he has killed many Boers at their farms during the last month, including women and children' (ibid, p. 122). Such successes clearly dismayed the Boer besiegers, especially as they had such major implications for the post-war social order. News of such white reverses at the hands of armed blacks probably also accounts for the increasing frequency and frantic nature of the protests and even threats communicated from Snyman, the local

Boer commander, to Baden-Powell. Snyman (like Cronje before him) continued to stress the extreme dangers of deploying armed blacks. Baden-Powell's repeated angry rejections of the protest did not just reflect his awareness of the hypocrisy of the Boer case (the Boers continued to deploy armed cattle guards around Mafeking defence lines). As long as such raids were crucial to the survival of the garrison, Baden-Powell was clearly now prepared to bypass the normal imperatives of social order. As Maj. Baillie succinctly confirmed: 'This success has naturally much pleased the natives and encouraged them greatly for future raids, which is most useful as the results feed us and harass the Boers' (Baillie, 13 March 1900, *Siege*, p. 176). Other African and black groups also distinguished themselves. Mr Algie noted in his diary one day: 'The Fingos came back from their looting expedition with five head of cattle' and the Baralongs this time were 'not successful – they were only able to capture one donkey' (Algie Diary, 23 March 1900). However, this is not to say that the Boers did not have their own successes. In early April, owing to a Boer ambush only four returned alive out of a thirty-strong Fingo 'looting expedition' (ibid, 8 April 1900).

In the frontline trenches even more spectacular successes were scored by the European-led African contingent 'Mackenzie's Boys', whose raid one night on Jackal Tree resulted in the death of 'one Boer and an African', and the capture of three horses and a number of rifles (Baillie, 17 March 1900, *Siege*, p. 178). Of all the black and African contingents, the much-admired Cape Boys, known for their precision shooting and outstanding loyalty (they constituted most of the garrison execution squads), were perhaps the most daring. They engaged in frequent verbal confrontations with their Boer protagonists, often accompanied by racial taunts. One incident involved the staging of a mock entertainment, in which the Cape Boys danced and called on the Boers to send them some of their ladies. This 'so chafed the Boers' that 'one of them, either attracted by the music or bursting with repartee, popped up his head and was incontinently shot by a wily Cape Boy'. The admiring but somewhat shocked Maj. Baillie commented: 'They have a distinct sense of humour, though possibly a somewhat grim one' (ibid, 8 April 1900).

If there were black heroes, then there were also black victims. By the end of March it was clear that the food situation for significant numbers of Africans trapped within the garrison perimeter was becoming critical. By early March deaths from starvation had become commonplace. On 12 March Algie reported how one European, Wenham, had found 'two natives who had died from starvation' (Algie Diary, 12 March 1900). Government soup kitchens expanded rapidly, with Plaatje noting the afternoon queues of 'hundreds of natives' at the nearby government kitchen (Plaatje, Mafeking Diary, p. 118). In March, Ross also observed how 'the lower class of natives' were 'beginning to suffer the pangs of starvation very severely: one poor devil was found on the south outskirts of the town this afternoon terribly emaciated and had to be carried to the hospital where they gave him a good feed' (Ross Diary, 9 March 1900). A significant and distressing sign of large-scale starvation was the recourse to the consumption of stray dogs as well as horse meat. Mr Ross recorded sympathetically, if a little patronisingly, one heart-rending scene that he witnessed after the weekly cull of stray dogs by the Town Ranger:

> The natives congregate in crowds as soon as one poor dog is shot … it resembles a children's school treat when sweets are thrown; they make a frantic rush and almost tear the carcass to pieces in their haste to obtain possession. The next moment it is in their cooking pots and eaten half raw. (ibid, 25 March 1900)

There were other desperate attempts by starving Africans to supplement the mainly horse meat and sowen diet. For example, on 15 March it was tersely reported how two men, Grayson and Stewart, on a journey through the *stadt* found 'starving natives eating the following: "crabs" [fresh water crayfish]; ox hide; dead dog' (Algie Diary, 15 March 1900).

Top: Africans shooting dogs for food. (Dr E.J. Yorke Collection)
Bottom: Africans waiting for their rations of horse meat soup. (Dr E.J Yorke Collection)

As more soup kitchens were opened to cope with the increasing crisis, there was some contemporary, if misplaced, criticism. For instance, Hamilton deplored the charging of threepence for each bowl of soup (Hamilton, *Siege*, p. 249). Neilly painted a particularly desperate situation, observing:

> I saw them fall down on the veldt and lie where they had fallen, too weak to go on their way. The sufferers … who were mostly little boys… Hunger had them in its grip and many of them were black spectres and living skeletons … their ribs literally breaking their shrivelled skin – men, women and children. Probably hundreds died from starvation or disease that always accompanies famine. Certain it is that many were found dead on the veldt. (Neilly, *Besieged*, pp. 227–9)

A closer examination of the sources, however, reveals that, as Tim Jeal has already indicated, starvation amongst the black population was by no means universal and the authorities were not wholly inactive as both contemporary and more recent critics such as Brian Gardner (Gardner, *Mafeking*, pp. 154–7) and Thomas Pakenham (Pakenham, *Boer War*, pp. 405–9) have suggested. In fact, by far the heaviest mortality rate was almost certainly experienced by the largely homeless Transvaal 'Uitlander group', encompassing the Zambesians and Shangaanis. Mr Algie states emphatically that 'the starving natives were principally Shangaans' (Algie Diary, 16 March 1900). When Plaatje witnessed another similar dog-culling scene on 15 March, it was highly significant that it was 'our local Zambesian friends' who 'unearth them immediately the ranger's assistants left the scene, and promptly cooked them for dinner, which gave the Baralong sections of the community the impression that there is more in a dog than they were ever told there was' (Plaatje, Mafeking Diary, p. 119). Even Neilly confirms after his harrowing description that 'the Baralongs proper were not so badly off; the least fortunate were the strange natives who came in from the Transvaal as refugees when the war started and the slaves and servants of the Baralong nation' (Neilly, *Besieged*, p. 230).

This last phrase also helps to explain why this effectively isolated group also suffered disproportionately. It is clear from many sources that little aid or support was provided for them by the permanent black residents. Indeed, Baillie noted the high degree of antipathy existing between the established Baralong community and these itinerant groups: 'The Shangaans … were detested by the other natives and consequently it is very hard to look after them properly … so much so that on Mr Vere ordering his Basuto servant to make some soup for a starving Shangaan he had picked up, the Basuto indignantly protested' (Baillie, 15 March 1900, *Siege*, pp. 209–10). Plaatje similarly noted how the majority of the soup kitchen refugees were 'made-up of the blackish races of this continent – mostly Zulus and Zambesians [who] venerate the Civil Commissioner and call me "bgwana molimo" [young god]'. He continued:

> It is really pitiful to see one who was too unfortunate to hear soon
> enough that there was a residency in Mafeking, and, being too
> weak to work, never had a chance to steal anything during the last
> six days, and so had nothing to eat … it was a miserable scene to be
> surrounded by about 50 hungry beings, agitating the engagement
> of your pity and to see one of them succumb to his agonies and fall
> back wards with a dead thud. (Plaatje, Mafeking Diary, pp. 124–5)

Final confirmation that *mass* starvation was confined to the
minority 'Transvaal African' groups was provided by a, perhaps,
more impartial observer, Lady Sarah Wilson. She supplied further
damning evidence on black divisions, confirming again 'the
Johannesburg tribes [who] were the ones to suffer most from
hunger in spite of Government relief and the fact that they had
plenty of money for they had done most of the trench work and
had been well paid' (Wilson, *Memories*, p. 101). She continued:
'… the reason was that they were strangers to the other natives
who had their own gardens to supplement their food allowance…
blacks are strangely unkind and hard to each other and remain
quite unmoved if a [to them] unknown man dies of starvation
although he be of their own colour' (ibid).

Moreover, it is also possible that these Transvaal African victims
numbered significantly fewer than has been hitherto suggested.
Algie noted on 16 March that 'since the 27th February exodus
approximately 1,000 had left town for the North' (Algie Diary,
16 March 1900). Similarly, on 17 March Plaatje confided that there
were in fact 'very few Shangaanis and Zambesians and the majority
had left this place and gone up country' (Plaatje, Mafeking Diary,
p. 120). On 22 March a thorough census of the *stadt* by Plaatje and
his white colleagues revealed 'no fewer than 5,448 people in the
stadt out of 10,000 at the commencement of hostilities … as quite
half the population have been clearing out in fours and fives as the
tension became more and more strained' (ibid, p. 125).

For the Baralong themselves, while food was undoubtedly
in short supply, most survived and a few even prospered in the

artificial market conditions created by the siege. As Lady Wilson observed, many Baralongs cultivated extensive vegetable gardens from which even the European townspeople were supplied, albeit at rising costs, giving 'an impression of prosperity' (Wilson, *Memories*, p. 101). On occasion fresh produce could even be obtained from outside the garrison defences. Plaatje noted on 9 March how some African women 'went out in the direction of Signal Hill to gather green makotone etc from their fields'; a touching scene in which racial animosity was unusually absent as 'young Boers … told them to glean in haste and return before their parents came as they would not permit them to take away any' (Plaatje, Mafeking Diary, p. 114). Later, on 13 March, Plaatje noted the often less stringent Boer cordons as 'women are now always going out to Moleloane [a village 5 miles north-west of Mafeking] and coming home with lots of melons and kaffir corn… we are wondering why the Boers permit them to go out as, for a while, they had not previously even been allowing them to get bushes for fuel behind the Convent on Sundays' (ibid, p. 116).

For the Baralongs in particular, an even richer source of income came from shares in the proceeds of the many cattle raids. Mr Algie noted the 'generous scale of rewards allocated by Colonel after one successful cattle raid by Mathlagong and 40 natives. This included £1 to £14 per head for 'recovering strange animals under fire' and for enemy's stock brought in 'one quarter belonged to the Government the remainder to be purchased by the Government at full price' (Algie Diary, 5 April 1900). Within the *stadt* itself, illegal horse-trading and cattle trading was widely prevalent, with significant cash sums exchanged. On occasions, even government interference was defied. When Baden-Powell reprimanded the normally compliant Lekoko for 'slaughtering some plundered cattle' without giving the Commissariat the chance of buying them, Lekoko's reply was: 'No *Cooler* … we have been giving you a fourth of all the loot and you said you did not care for it' (Plaatje, Mafeking Diary, p. 101). Other Baralong who owned fowls became heavily engaged in a thriving egg trade, with eggs fetching sixpence each (Baillie, 7 February 1900, *Siege*, p. 127). Indeed, the amount of coinage retained in African hands was cited by Baden-Powell and others as the main reason for the resort to the issue of siege paper currency earlier in March of that year (Baden-Powell, 10 March 1900, Staff Diary, BPP).

There were other ingenious strategies for survival. Several Africans took advantage of the thriving trade in shell cases eagerly purchased by the Europeans as souvenirs. Ada Cock recalled how a 'Big Ben' shell that 'came over the base and stuck in the mud was picked up by a "Kaffir" and sold … for £6' (Cock, *Petticoat in Mafeking*, p. 64). Other lucrative sources of employment included carrying blankets for European troops, for which 'African "blanket boys" were paid one sixpence and part of their rations' (Plaatje, Mafeking Diary, p. 83). On rare occasions 'mother nature' provided a welcome helping hand. In late March a massive swarm of locusts provided a major supplement to African diets, with Mr Algie noting that 'because of the locust swarm there were not so many natives at the soup kitchens' (Algie Diary, 23 March 1900).

The locust which Europeans were compelled by hunger to eat during the Siege of Mafeking. (Dr E.J. Yorke Collection)

Lady Sarah Wilson and her 'dug-out'. (Dr E.J. Yorke Collection)

For the much-valued African political and military elites, life was much more bearable – for example, by Government Notice 192, 'natives bearing arms were given regular rations, including one quart of sowen daily' (ibid, 11 April 1900). Educated Africans, such as court interpreter Plaatje, survived on often quite generous weekly government rations that included groceries (tea, coffee, sugar, pepper and salt), vegetables (green mealies, beet, cabbage, turnips and carrots etc., from the gardens and fields on the riverbeds), and preserved meat (Plaatje, Mafeking Diary, pp. 126–7).

A good indicator, however, of the growing distress amongst some, especially the minority alien African groups, was the rising crime rate. Theft became a key strategy for survival and, from early March onwards, the crime rate within Mafeking soared. Many of these perpetrators of thefts, especially in the gardens of the *stadt* and the European residential areas, were again mostly Shangaans. Thus, a nervous Ada Cock noted with alarm both their culpability and the close links with the ongoing food crisis, which escalated into wild rumours of cannibalism:

> There were a lot of Shangaans under the trees here and they had been stealing my fowls. I have only nine left. They are dying of starvation. I don't know what they had been living on but the smell is something dreadful. They had been moved up to the empty Police Barracks and are killing and eating all the dogs they can get. Arthur [the caretaker] says he believes they ate their dead chum who was never carted away… someone said he smelt human flesh roasting. It is quite dangerous to let children run about by themselves. I don't know' (Cock, *Petticoat in Mafeking,* p. 65).

Hamilton also remarked on the growing phenomena of domestic animal thefts with 'natives … at their wits end [having] resorted to a variety of dishes which under more favourable circumstances they would not touch. Pet dogs which are sleek, family cats that are fat, are stolen nightly from the hotels and empty houses… they are invariably traced to native marauders who, inspired by hunger, prowl around by night seeking what they might devour' (Hamilton, *Siege*, p. 288).

The rising crime rate was reflected in Plaatje's own court records, in which theft of fuel and food cases predominated (four out of seven listed on 20 March court sitting). The defendants were invariably 'foreign natives'. The cases arraigned included an old Zulu 'charged with stealing wood' and, significantly, an 'old miserable half-starved Shangaan charged with theft of green mealies … [notably] the property of the Chief Lekoko'. The latter's plea was 'guilty under provocation – hunger'. On 29 March yet another Shangaan was charged with the theft of a horse; his plea was 'guilty under provocation' as he had been living on 'thepe', a type of vegetable (Plaatje, Mafeking Diary, pp. 122–3). 'Foreign natives' caught stealing in the *stadt* gardens could receive rough justice. 'One heathen' caught 'stealing garden produce' was 'nearly beaten to death' by a Baralong mob – yet another testament to the growing inter-African friction (ibid, p. 105).

The penalties for theft became progressively harsher and, by early April, repeated theft had become a capital offence. On 2 April, for instance, 'a native' twice found guilty of theft was executed at sundown, again by a firing party of six Cape Boys (Ross Diary, 2 April 1900). Others received heavy floggings for first offences. Social control was also tightened. Already from 8 February onwards, as the food crisis escalated, 'no natives were allowed in town without a pass'. Three 'classes' of Africans were established – permanent town employees, permanent employees outside town and *stadt* folk. Each received coloured tickets in the same manner as in Kimberley, and this may have helped control the crime rate as pass violators could be brought before the courts (Plaatje, Mafeking Diary, p. 96).

These two desperate months constituted perhaps the most controversial period in Baden-Powell's career. Critics have accused him not only of discriminatory rationing practices, but also of deliberate neglect of emergency food supplies for the African population. However, these can again be seriously contended. As Jeal pointed out, although 'BP' was by no means even-handed in his food distribution, with superior rations allocated to both black elite groups and Europeans as a whole, even Neilly, the most vociferous contemporary critic, concedes that, as early as March, when Baden-Powell 'got to know of the state of affairs he instituted soup kitchens ... where horses were boiled in huge caldrons and the savoury mess doled out in pints and quarts to all comers' (Neilly, *Besieged*, pp. 228–9). Significantly, 'some of the people – those employed on the works – paid for food: the remainder who were in the majority obtained it free' (ibid). This corrected Hamilton's earlier criticism of compulsory food payments for all Africans. On 20 March, Algie recorded an increasingly rapid response to the African food crisis with 'the distribution of food … reorganised and everyone had something to eat' (Algie Diary, 20 March 1900). Indeed, '[by direct order of Baden-Powell] about 30 half-starved Shangaans were put into the Cape Police stables and looked after there' (ibid). By 14 March, Baden-Powell showed his direct and growing concern by recording, on 14 March, the establishment of a board 'to consider question of feeding the natives and suggesting any improvement' (Baden-Powell, 14 March 1900, Staff Diary). Moreover, it is probable that some of the earlier recorded harsher measures, such as excessive charging for soup, were unofficially adopted by junior officers or administrators attached to the kitchens and without the knowledge of the ever-busy Baden-Powell. Hence the comment by Col Hore, one of the more humanitarian presiding judges who expressed sympathy towards many theft defendants, who specifically blamed the 'soup kitchen people' for those 'shameful deeds … they don't feed the people at all'. In the event, by mid to late April, as Ross, himself often critical of Baden-Powell, confirmed: 'BP has done everything he could to alleviate distress among the natives none of whom need now starve … if they are not too lazy to walk as far as the horse meat soup kitchens' (Ross Diary, 23 April 1900).

The total number of deaths from starvation amongst the African population will never be accurately known. A terrible tragedy did occur, but the overall mortality rate, as Plaatje's census figures would suggest, can be counted in the few hundreds rather than thousands. Moreover, any situation approaching mass starvation only occurred amongst the trapped and relatively isolated Transvaal African groups, particularly the Shangaanis, of whom it would seem only about 500 remained within the town precincts by the end of March – a statistic that corresponds to Jeal's figures (Jeal, *Baden-Powell*, p. 272). After the obvious mistake of the enforced exodus of these groups in late February and the subsequent disastrous failure, it can be argued that Baden-Powell did make strenuous efforts to alleviate the deteriorating conditions of those left behind. Indeed, Plaatje, the sole recorded African voice from the siege, laid no blame at the door of Baden-Powell: his finger of guilt pointed solely at those 'abominable Transvaal Boers', who had driven these unfortunate people into the Mafeking compounds at the start of the siege (Plaaatje, Mafeking Diary, p. 125). Indeed, in a public letter published in the *Mafeking Mail* at the end of March, Baden-Powell himself resolutely defended his rationing policies to both his European and African critics, such as Lekoko. Contrasting his admittedly relatively harsh regime with the far worse prospects of Boer captivity, he wrote:

> As regards the smallness of our rations we could of course live well on full rations for a week or two and then give in to the 'women slaughterers' and let them take their vengeance on the town whereas by limiting our amount of daily food we can make certain of outlasting all their efforts against us. The present ration, properly utilised, is a fairly full one as compared with those issued in other sieges. (Baden-Powell, *Mafeking Mail*, 30 March 1900)

While aspects of Baden-Powell's 'social policies' during the siege will no doubt remain controversial, in other spheres he proved himself an exceptional political and military leader. Even at the most pressurised times during the critical months of 1900, European and African morale continued to be sustained by his ingenious and original morale building exercises. Sunday concerts and entertainments were conducted even in the midst of enemy bombardment. On Sunday 5 April, for instance, the garrison was treated to a volunteer sports display by the Bechuanaland Rifles and a fancy dress competition (Algie Diary, 15 April 1900). Moreover, contrary to the claims of his critics, Baden-Powell did often praise and reward the individual exploits of his African as well as his white defenders. For example, on 11 April, from his famous 'lookout position', Baden-Powell observed:

> A very plucky bit of native work when an exceptionally brave African herd boy, under deliberately targeted Boer shell fire (combined nine-pounder and one-pounder Maxim fire), successfully rounded up and rescued a large section of the garrison's herd of horses. The colonel promptly rewarded the boy with a £5 note. (Ross Diary, 11 April 1900)

Again, when twenty of 'Abraham's Boys' successfully defeated a 150-strong massed Boer attack on the Brickfields trenches 'letting them have two or three volleys' and 'bowling over four or five of the enemy', Baden-Powell mentioned all of them in General Orders that very same evening (ibid). On 14 April Baden-Powell also fulsomely praised and rewarded Baralong raiders at an indaba with Chief Lekoko and his assembled headmen (Baden-Powell, 14 April 1900, Staff Diary). White as well as black youths also performed sterling tasks. As mentioned earlier, the Cadet Corps, supervised by Lord Edward Cecil and made up of white boys over the age of 9 but too young for full military service, acted, often under heavy shellfire, as messengers, postmen and orderlies, providing inspiration for Baden-Powell's later establishment of the Boy Scout Movement.

Above all, regardless of his critics, there is little doubt that Baden-Powell's personal qualities and his indomitable spirit provided the ultimate source of inspiration for the defenders of Mafeking. Hamilton has provided a rare but vivid appreciation of Baden-Powell at the height of his powers; one which, while exposing his undoubted egotism, also reveals his special mesmeric qualities, including his stoicism and unrelenting sense of duty that made him such an effective military leader:

> Colonel Baden-Powell is young, as men go in the Army, with a keen appreciation of the possibilities of his career, swayed by ambition, indifferent to sentimental emotion. In stature his is short, while his features are sharp and smooth. He is eminently a man of determination, of great physical endurance and capacity, and of extraordinary reticence. His reserve is unbending ... he

does not go about freely since he is tied to his office through the multitudinous cares of his command and he is chiefly happy when he can snatch the time to escape on one of those nocturnal, silent expeditions, which alone calm and assuage the perpetual excitement of his present existence. Outwardly, he maintains an impenetrable screen of self-control, observing with a cynical smile the foibles and caprices of those around him. He seems ever bracing himself to be on guard against a moment in which he should be swept by some unnatural and spontaneous enthusiasm, in which by a word, by an expression of face, by a movement, or in the turn of a phrase, he should betray the rigours of the self-control under which he lives. Every passing townsman regards him with curiosity not unmixed with awe. Every servant in the hotel watches him, and he, as a consequence, seldom speaks without a preternatural deliberation and an air of decisive finality. He seems to close every argument with a snap, as though the steel manacles of his ambition had checkmated the emotions of the man in the instincts of the officer. He weighs each remark before he utters it, suggests by his manner, as by his words, that he has considered the different effects it might conceivably have on any mind at the expression of his own mind. As an officer, he has given to Mafeking a complete and assured security, to the construction of which he has brought a very practical knowledge of the conditions of Boer warfare, of the Boers themselves and of the strategic worth of the adjacent areas. His espionage excursions to the Boer lines have gained him an intimate and accurate knowledge of the value of the opposing forces and a mass of data by which he can immediately counteract the enemy's attack. He loves the night, and after his return from the hollows in the veldt, where he has kept many anxious vigils, he lies awake hour after hour upon his camp mattress in the veranda, tracing out in his mind, the various means and agencies by which he can forestall their move, which unknown to them, he has personally watched … As he makes his way across our lines the watchful sentry strains his eyes a little more to keep the figure of the Colonel before him, until the undulations of the veldt conceal his progress … He goes on never faltering, bending for a moment behind a clump of rocks, screening himself next behind some bushes, crawling upon his hands and knees, until his movements, stirring a few loose stones, create a thin grating noise in the vast silence about him. His head is low, his eyes gaze straight upon the camp of the enemy; in a little he moves again, his inspection is over, and he either changes to a fresh point or startles some dozing sentry as he slips back into town. (Hamilton, *Siege*, pp. 192–5)

However, there was one 'spectre of death' – disease – which was beyond even Baden-Powell's considerable powers of control. As mentioned earlier in February, outbreaks of diphtheria and dysentery had been reported and, by 10 March, Algie had reported 'typhoid amidst the whites with smallpox and scurvy amongst the natives' (Algie Diary, 10 March 1900). The enforced confinement of the defenders and the extreme state of malnutrition had ensured that, by the end of March, 12.5 per cent of the garrison had been hospitalised owing to sickness, disease and casualties (Ross Diary, 30 March 1900). These figures do not include the many bedridden victims confined at home or those many unknown African victims in the *stadt* area. At the end of April, Hamilton reported both its rapid spread and the devastating impact on garrison morale as 'fever flags' floated over designated quarantine areas within the township:

There are three such places; one is remote from our lines, well out into the veldt where it is not permitted to go, where … isolated and apart … is a family fighting against the ravages of diphtheria; between them and the stadt there is a smallpox reserve where a yellow jack droops from the trees behind whose shadows the tents of the patients have been pitched. Still nearer into town and nearer the hospital the flag of mercy protects that building in which there is much malaria, some typhoid and a few cases of enteric fever… It is in these quarters that we, who are hale and hearty, look with anxious eyes. There are many here that will pay with their lives as tributes to the Siege. (Hamilton, *Siege*, p. 287; see also Algie Diary, 16 March 1900)

It was an excessively gloomy but fitting epitaph to over six and a half months of mounting ordeal for the defenders of Mafeking.

Phase 3: The Relief and 'Reconquest' of Mafeking, April–June 1900

1900		
	9 April	Roberts again telegraphs Baden-Powell to postpone relief to 10 June
	12 May	Failed final 'Eloff' Boer attack – many Boer prisoners taken; others massacred by Baralong
	17 May	Relief of Mafeking
	Mid-May to end of June	Widespread social disorder. Mafeking garrison troops and local British troops restore stability in surrounding districts

Despite welcome news of the slow but steady progress of Col Plumer's relief force, the garrison approached the transition from April to May with a palpable sense of foreboding. Ross reported: 'The enemy's main laager grows bigger every day and it is now known that Commandant Eloff is in charge of the enemy outside and so an extra keen watch is being kept. He has brought large reinforcements and we may soon expect a good deal of fighting' (Ross Diary, 29–30 April 1900). The 'dashing fellow' Sarel Eloff (1863–1924), renowned for his energy and aggression, had joined the Boer besiegers on 24 April, and as a field cornet and nephew of President Kruger he enjoyed a position of high status and prestige amongst his Boer compatriots. Ada Cock disconsolately reinforced the mood of gloom: 'People seem to think the relief will come some time about the end of the month but I do not like to think about it' (Cock, 6 May 1900, *Petticoat in Mafeking*, p. 89).

Eloff's attack on Mafeking: BSAP escorting Boer prisoners to the lock-up. (Dr E.J. Yorke Collection)

After its heaviest day of shelling on 11 April, the feared Boer artillery piece 'Big Ben' was withdrawn, having fired 13,379 shells or '65 tons of cast iron' (Ross Diary, 10 May 1900). While some comfort was expressed at this, there were other ominous signs of enhanced Boer determination, if not an imminent offensive. On Sunday 6 May the already fragile concept of a 'gentlemen's war' evaporated as the Boers demonstrated a new unprecedented degree of ruthlessness by directly attacking a BSAP funeral. An outraged Ada Cock observed how 'the Boers were volleying at the funeral procession, the bullets falling about 10 or 12 yards short. The funerals have always been at night but the Colonel thought he would have this one at seven in the morning and that is how the Boers behaved' (Cock, 6 May 1900, *Petticoat in Mafeking*, pp. 88–9). A grim Ross confirmed that this despicable act had 'destroyed all future Sunday truces. No more sports etc for us. Very hard luck' (Ross diary, 6 May 1900). By 9 May even 'white flag communication' had been broken off and, by then, an outraged

Baden-Powell had already promptly retaliated by ordering troops based at Fort Ayr and Fort Nelson to open continuous fire on the nearby Boer trenches (Baden-Powell, 6 May 1900, Staff Diary). Garrison morale was also hard-hit by news of the severe disablement of the 'black hero' Sgt Abrahams. He had been severely injured with Trooper Cook by an unexploded 94lb shell: '… his left foot … blown in half from the heel to instep just hanging by the skin' with, as Ada Cock remembered, 'the hot blood running all over my hands' (Cock, 6 May 1900, *Petticoat in Mafeking*, p. 89). Nevertheless, his African military compatriots continued to achieve successes. Thus, Ross observed how 'Mackenzie's native boys managed to bowl over two of the enemy this morning on the railway lines and since then kept them from recovering the bodies. They had no Red Cross flag so our men were perfectly justified' (Ross Diary, 6 May 1900). There was, it would seem, a new ruthless edge to this prolonged war of attrition.

Such small skirmishes and individual human losses were matched by the depressing scenes of desolation throughout the town. Collateral damage after over seven months of siege was now extensive. Scarcely a house was left undamaged. In early

Miss Craufurd and Mrs Buchan, the two ladies who, under Boer escort, carried food and medical supplies to the captive officers in Col Hore's fort under heavy fire. (Dr E.J. Yorke Collection)

May, Ross vividly recorded the 'Armageddon' atmosphere, in which parts of the town seemed to resemble a lunar landscape, and in which everyday life was conducted largely underground:

> Poor old Mafeking looks now a perfect hole of desolation; all the trees have been cut down for firewood, all the wooden fences torn up for a like purpose, the houses all in a state of complete wreckage. There is not a single house or store in the town that has not at some time or another been severely punished by shellfire, many having to be pulled down as being dangerous; all the galvanised iron roofs of those standing are riddled with shrapnel and bullets, until they resembled enormous corrugated sieves. Black gaping holes here, there, and everywhere, showing where the shell passed through on its way to other damage or to kill, kill, kill. The shop windows that have not fallen in are nailed up by pieces of old iron, packing cases or anything else that could be used. Here and there can be seen a huge tarpaulin spread over a roof, endeavouring to keep the inmates at least dry. The ends of all the streets barricaded by large, heavy sheets of galvanised iron supported by large heavy buck-waggons and sandbags. Miniature loopholed forts made of sandbags dotted here and there about the town at different corners of streets. Protection holes dug out of the streets all over the town. Not a solitary unbroken window to be seen, not even the little curl of homely smoke to be seen coming out of the few chimneys that are left. Hardly a soul, man, woman, or child, to be seen about the streets, and the very few one does meet are white, hungry, gaunt-looking faces that make one shudder, and give one the blues. The whole town gives me the impression that this is what it will look like at the time the poor old Earth has had her last shaking up and the last Trumpet has been blown. (Ross Diary, 10 May 1900)

The scale of destruction had already caused intense friction between Baden-Powell and elements of the civilian population.

As early as March, a wearying Baden-Powell had received angry letters from the Mafeking Town Council imploring him 'to consider the question of damages and losses sustained by the whole of Mafeking as a result of the Siege', and demanding 'substantial compensation' (Chamber of Commerce to Baden-Powell, 27 March 1900; enclosed in Ross Diary, 31 March 1900). By the end of March, he had, in typical blunt fashion, clamped down on this continual complaining. While reassuring them of imperial compensation, he warned:

> Grousing is generally the outcome of funk on the part of the individual who grouses, and I hope that every right-minded man who hears any of it will shut it up with an appropriate remark or toe of his boot. Cavillers should keep quiet until the Siege is over and then they are welcome to write or talk until they are blue in the face… there are few individual grumblers, most of whom are known to me… it is these gentlemen that I desire to warn to keep quiet otherwise I shall have to take more stringent steps against them, but I should be ashamed if the fame of Mafeking and its heroic defence were to be marred by a whisper among envious outsiders, that there was any want of harmony or unity of purpose amongst us. (Baden-Powell, 31 March 1900, Staff Diary; and Plaatje, Mafeking Diary, p. 133)

By the start of May, Baden-Powell had far more serious military matters to concern him. A telegram from Gen. Roberts on 9 April had again postponed the prospects for relief of the siege from 8 May to 10 June, plunging Baden-Powell into another unexpected ration crisis (Roberts to Baden-Powell, 9 April 1900; and Baden-Powell, 20 April 1900, Staff Diary, BPP). He was again forced to consider the unsavoury prospect of 'forcing natives away from Mafeking to save horse meat and save rations' (Baden-Powell, 20 April 1900, Staff Diary, BPP). In the same telegram, however, he demonstrated a degree of compassion and a determination to eventually compensate local Africans for any distress caused: 'suggest in concluding peace to fine Boers cattle and repay looted loyalists and natives' (ibid). A meeting held at the end of April with his key military confidants, Lord Cecil, Maj. Gould-Adams and Maj. Godley, revealed why Baden-Powell had again been forced into taking what might appear to have been unwarranted and extreme measures. By then the garrison's morale and fitness level had reached crisis point. The 'rush of sickness' combined with a cold snap and heavy rain had led to 'over 20 admissions to hospital in the previous 36 hours' (Baden-Powell, 21 April 1900). Dysentery, malaria and typhoid were rife, with the prospect of a major epidemic. Baden-Powell knew that without fit and able-bodied defenders there was no prospect of survival for anyone in the garrison. The conclusions of this meeting were uncompromising: 'We all agreed the men reduced in strength by the continuance of low diet… small extras they normally purchased to supplement their diet were now failing… sickness is beginning to tell – fever and dysentery becoming prevalent and that not only can no reduction in rations be made but rather an increase is desirable'. (*ibid*). In his otherwise very sparse and generalised 'memories' of the siege, Maj. Godley distinctly remembers this crisis meeting 'with Gould-Adams and Cecil, at which we decided that a further reduction in rations was out of the question. At the same time we realised that to increase them from our small reserve stock would mean that all supplies would be finished by the end of May' (Godley, *Life of an Irish Soldier*, pp. 80–1). Furthermore, in a stark warning to Col Plumer, head of the relief force, Baden-Powell asserted: 'health of the garrison can no longer go on to 10th June' (Baden-Powell, 25 April 1900, Staff Diary, BPP).

Moreover, contrary to both his contemporary and current critics, who accused him of perpetuating the siege for his own self-glorification, Baden-Powell did actively consider, in the face of this major crisis, 'withdrawing garrison, leaving civilians here'. Although this course of action would be 'undesirable in terms of loss or prestige, valuable property (including 18 locomotives)', he argued

*The convent, Mafeking, showing the damage wrought by Boer shells.
(Dr E.J. Yorke Collection)*

that 'tactically' the British cause would 'not lose much as we could
divert the enemy and even shut them up in Mafeking' (Baden-
Powell, 25 April 1900, Staff Diary, BPP). On 2 May Baden-Powell
reiterated: 'If our relief founders after all, I shall make an effort to
withdraw the garrison' (Baden-Powell, 2 May 1900, Staff Diary, BPP).

Furthermore, there was plenty of other ground-level evidence of
a crisis by early May 1900. For instance, horses were 'now dying of
poverty as fast as we can kill them for soup' and, on 10 May, Ross
tersely recalled even more drastic measures being taken: 'We have
now commenced soup kitchens for whites. The stuff is horrible but
we must live just a little bit longer' (Ross Diary, 10 May 1900). As
Baden-Powell, no longer confident of a firm relief date, desperately
held onto existing food stocks, further new 'survival diets' were
concocted, the most notorious being 'brawn', a meal ostensibly
invented by the Cape Boys from ox hides. Eventual ingredients
included 'horse hooves, heads, cowhide, donkey meat, carpenters
glue, spice and split peas'. Brawn was sold to Europeans at 1s a
pound, often to supplement sowen at sixpence a quart. As Ross
wryly commented: 'One cannot get through much of this but the

SIEGE SURVIVAL RATIONS:

	At First	Latterly
Meat	1lb	¾lb to 1lb
Bread	1lb	5oz
Vegetables	1lb	6oz
Coffee	⅓oz	⅓oz
Salt	½oz	½oz
Sugar	2oz	
Tea	½oz	
Sowen	1 quart	

(Source: HMSO, *Mafeking*, p. 171)

natives seem to appreciate it highly and get full up with it. I think everything in this place has been eaten except horseshoes and barbed wire.' Such was the scarcity that one 'artful Johnny' who had secreted a fowl in his dugout managed to sell it for 30s. (ibid)

Amongst the Mafeking African population, small pockets of starvation were still evident and were again illustrated by continually high crime levels. Both Baralongs and Europeans were forced to guard their cattle herds closely, the numbers of which had remained relatively constant, largely owing to the continuing success of the garrison's African cattle raiders. On 28 April, Ada Cock recorded the dangers at night in the midst of an internal crime wave as 'the starving niggers are jumping cattle' (Cock, 28 April 1900, *Petticoat in Mafeking*, p. 98). By 3 May she had resorted to desperate measures to protect her remaining cattle stocks after:

> some natives stole granny's beautiful little cow… I let Willie [the caretaker] know at once and the Government sent detectives out. She was found yesterday half eaten. They have three boys in the trunk, two got away or rather they could not catch them. So now I have my revolver loaded and Willie has had chains made and put the chains around the wagon wheel and then padlocked it around their necks. The native will have to kill them here if they want to now and then I will hear and give them a small pill! (ibid)

For many others, notably the Baralong cattle raiding fraternity, opportunity was still rife. As Baden-Powell lamented, even the newly instituted government sequestration operations to conserve food were being thwarted as 'natives whose stock disappeared … had sent them away … to avoid having them commandeered'.

African woman escaping through the Boer lines. (Dr E.J. Yorke Collection)

The colonel was forced to have 'all stock taken over by the ASC and put under our herds under Mr Whitfield' (Baden-Powell, 1 May 1900, Staff Diary, BPP).

In the midst of such trials and tribulations there were still occasional bouts of sardonic humour. Thus, one communication sent by Eloff, the Boer commander, to Baden-Powell, noting the garrison's regular Sunday habit of playing cricket matches, asked permission to bring a team into town one Sunday for a friendly game. This elicited the reply by the eternally sharp-witted Baden-Powell that, although the garrison was over 200 (days) not out, it had not yet closed its innings and he had better try to get a change of bowlers! (Baden-Powell, 30 April 1900, Staff Diary, BPP)

On 12 May the Mafeking 'wicket' almost fell as Eloff and 300-odd Boer fighters launched the much-feared and anticipated attack on the enervated garrison.

Mr B. Weil, the man who fed Mafeking. (Dr E.J. Yorke Collection)

The attack has been briefly examined elsewhere, but it is worth examining key episodes to illustrate both the traumatic personal and individual experiences of this last major struggle for survival and the hitherto neglected role of the African auxiliaries who again demonstrated heroism equal to that of their white compatriots, as well as an extraordinary capacity for all-out merciless revenge against their hated Boer enemy. The attack can be separated into three distinct phases. The first comprised the surprised foray into the town via the African *stadt* and the capture of the BSAP fort, including Col Hore and twenty-two BSAP, at around 5.50 a.m. Secondly, the counter-offensive when Baden-Powell conducted a stoic defence, directing Maj. Godley, another hero of the siege, to cut off Eloff in the fort and round up the increasingly isolated Boer outposts within the *stadt*. Lastly, there was the final phase comprising the recapture of the BSAP fort and the controversial 'mopping up operations' that followed.

During the first phase the huge shock delivered to an already severely weakened Mafeking garrison was graphically evident. Widespread panic ensued amongst both black and white Mafeking citizens. Ada Cock recalled those terrible moments at around 4 a.m. on Saturday 12 May:

> It has been an awful morning – somehow the enemy have got into the BSAP [BSA Police] camp about 500 yards from here… Willie and all of us got up at 4.30, hearing terrible firing and bugles blowing… Soon, one end of the stadt was blazing and the niggers running and screaming… (Cock, 12 May 1900, *Petticoat in Mafeking*, pp. 99–101)

Lady Wilson feared the worst as Mafeking's defences were suddenly so dangerously exposed:

> The Boers in the stadt! Such was the ominous message that quickly passed around … as day was breaking. One had to be well acquainted with the labyrinth of rocks, trees, huts and

cover generally … all within a stone's throw of our dwelling to realise the dread import of these words… the moon had just set and it was pitch dark. The firearm fusillade first began from the east and when I opened the door on to the step the din was terrific, while swish, swish came the bullets just beyond the cover blinds nailed to the edge of the veranda to keep off the sun. Now and then the boom of a small gun varied the noise but the rifles never ceased for an instant! To this awe-inspiring tune I dressed by the light of a carefully shaded candle to avoid giving any mark for our foes… In various stages of dishabille the people were running around the house searching for rifles, fowling pieces and even sticks as weapons of defence. (Wilson, *Memories*, pp. 204–5)

Baillie witnessed the terrible scenes in the *stadt* as Baralong men, women and children were ruthlessly shot down and up to forty huts set alight:

Suddenly on the west a conflagration was seen and betting began as to how far out it was. I got onto the roof of a house, and with Mr Arnold, saw a very magnificent sight … the whole stadt was on fire and with sunrise behind us the stadt in flames in front, the combination of effects was magnificent, if not exactly reassuring! (Baillie, 15 May 1900, *Siege*, p. 253)

Ross testified to the intensity of Boer rifle fire:

Bullets fell like hailstones all over the town, the Market Square at times having the appearance of being lit up with electric sparks caused by explosive bullets or the Mauser bullet striking bits of stone or flint… I shall never forget the run I had from our place in this Market Square to the fort I was attached at to Early's Corner. How I dodged those bullets God alone knows. They were under me, over me, all around me, so I suppose I was meant for something else. (Ross Diary, 13 May 1900)

In these desperate moments even the town jail, 400yd from the BSAP fort, was emptied of prisoners, including convicted murderer Lt Murchison and convicted black marketer Sgt Looney, and issued with rifles, the only predictable exception being the three Dutch prisoners. Ross thus encountered on the roof 'poor old Murchison firing away for all he was worth with an old Martini rifle we had taken from one of the police prisoner guards. He, at any rate, was pleased at his temporary liberty and said he did not care a damn … whether he was shot or not' (ibid).

At this critical time, between 5 p.m. and 7.30 p.m., Baden-Powell again demonstrated his exceptional military leadership by swiftly and coolly establishing order and rapidly reorganising the defences to close the dangerous gap caused by the Boer incursion. In this second phase of the battle, Maj. Godley emerged as yet another garrison hero, as, under telephoned orders from Baden-Powell, he courageously led units of the Protectorate Regiment, BSAP and elements of the Cape Police from the Brickfields and Cannon Kopje to re-establish the broken defence lines and cut off the captured BSAP fort and Eloff's withdrawal route. Maj. Godley described his desperate ride to link up with these reassembled units and thus plug the gap. As 'officers were galloping around everywhere', Godley recalled, 'my difficulty was to get the squadrons assembled … I decided that the best thing to do was to concentrate as best we could on the south side of the stadt and then drive in from east and west and so cut off those Boers who had got into the fort from the parties who had remained in the stadt'. It was a desperate ride, as 'to get to the rendezvous I had to go out in front of our defences and gallop around across the Molopo River and outside the stadt. After I had crossed the river I was well sniped at from the stadt, but I had managed to keep my pony (one of the few remaining in the garrison in fairly good condition) and made my pace so fast that I evidently presented a rather difficult running target; the bullets whistled either over or behind me. Our drive was entirely successful' (Godley, *Life of an Irish Soldier,* p. 81).

Sowen

Another food innovation was sowen, a form of porridge made from the fermented bran of oats after the flour had been extracted for making bread. 100lb of bran in 37 gallons of water give 33 gallons of sowen. 'On this food,' Baden-Powell asserts, 'we fed both natives and whites'. There were five sowen kitchens, each capable of producing 800 gallons daily. It was sold at 6*d* per quart to those not entitled to a ration.

(Source: Baden-Powell to CSO to Lord Roberts, 18 May 1900, enclosed in HMSO, *Mafeking*, p. 180)

The considerably grimmer final phase of this battle now began. The last stands of the now surrounded Boers in the *stadt* were mostly only overcome after furious firefights. The confidence of the garrison's defenders rapidly returned. Baillie witnessed 'bodies of men, individuals, everybody armed with what they could get, guns of any sort, running towards the firing, a smile on every man's face and the usual remark was, "now we've got the beggars"' (Baillie, 15 May 1900, *Siege*, p. 253). Small units of Boer fighters, often laden with loot, made desperate attempts to escape. Baillie again noticed 'one clumpy' of Boers who:

> galloped forth laden with food and drink. The food belonged to them; the drink belonged to us. They happened to fall in with a galloping Maxim, a piece of bad luck because they all died and our people took the food and drink. One fellow had taken a pair of brown boots and a horse; he had a few bullets through the boots, the horse was killed and so was he. (Ibid)

A steady trickle of captured Boer wounded arrived at the garrison's field hospitals. Nurse Craufurd's heroic work has already been mentioned, but the redoubtable Lady Wilson also bore witness to the 'gruesome sight seeing the wounded brought in and the bloody stretchers carried away empty', while the wounded Boer prisoners 'begged not to have sheets, as they had never seen such things before'. It was also left to Lady Wilson to comfort one of the few British casualties, the mortally wounded Staff Orderly Hazelrigg of the Cape Police. As he 'bled to death ... I sat with him for several hours, putting eau de cologne on his head and brushing away the flies. In the evening, just before he passed into unconsciousness, he repeated more than once, "Tell the Colonel, Lady Sarah, I did my best to give the message, but they got me first". He died at dawn' (Wilson, *Memories*, pp. 208–9).

Hazelrigg's valiant death, which occurred in a desperate attempt to carry Baden-Powell's messages to beleaguered parts of the garrison, had an equally profound effect on Baden-Powell, as had

SIEGE COMMUNICATIONS

A. Local

1. Telephone: all outlying forts and look-out posts were connected up with HQ, managed by the postmaster, Mr Howat, and his staff.

2. Postal: to cover the heavy expenses of runners, and for the convenience of the public, postage was established at 1*d* for town, 3*d* for outlying forts and 1*s* for up country.

3. Signalling: heliograph, lamp and flag signalling were established for defence purposes by brigade signallers under Maj. Panzera and Sgt Maj. Moffat. Megaphones were made and used in out-lying trenches and posts. Phonophores were also made and used on the armoured train, attached to ordinary telegraph lines.

B: Distant

Runners: African runners were deployed twice weekly, or more often when necessary, to take despatches and letters to the northern relief column. Baden-Powell observed: 'They had to be highly paid, as the risk of capture and death was very great.'
(Source: HMSO, *Mafeking*, p. 163)

McLaren's grievous wounding earlier in the siege. It reinforces the more plausible explanation that Baden-Powell's bond with these men was based on military comradeship and shared duty rather than any recently suggested implications of homosexuality.

It was at this stage of the attack that the African contribution, particularly by the Baralongs in the *stadt* area, became evident. They played a courageous role in both isolating and overwhelming the last Boer defenders. Baden-Powell himself noted how 'the Baralong had acted as scouts and found out where the remaining [Boers] had posted themselves' (Baden-Powell, Staff Diary, BPP). Trooper Saunders of the reinforcing Bechuanaland Rifles also significantly recalled how, 'Baralongs from the stadt ran into town reporting that the Boers had passed through their kraals' (Saunders, *Mafeking Memories*, p. 112). Baillie gave enormous credit to the Baralong support in isolating scattered Boer positions, singling out for particular praise the efforts of Lekoko and Silas Molema, who had tactically decided that it was 'better to kraal them [the Boers] up like cattle' (Baillie, 15 May 1900, *Siege*, p. 263). He noted: '… this species of fighting particularly appeals to the Baralong. He is better than the Boer at the Boers' own game and never will I hear a word against the Baralong' (ibid).

Thus, with the help of the already rearmed Baralong scouting guide, it was soon discovered that thirty-odd Boer fighters were penned-up in a stone kraal (cattle enclosure) and fifty-odd in a rocky limestone koppie (small hill). In the final capture of these two main positions, the Baralong again played a significant, if somewhat ominous, role. Two dozen Boers hemmed-in at the 'koppie' surrendered under Maj. Godley's final threat of instant death (the garrison's 7lb gun had been lined up at point blank range!). At that moment, a Capt. Marsh 'at fearful risk jumped in amongst them and interposed himself between the cowering Boers and their would-be murderers' (*Mafeking Mail*, 14 May 1900). The hunger of the garrison troops was immediately evident as the captured enemy haversacks, with four days' rations of bread and biltong (cured meat), were 'soon made short work of'

(Ross Diary, 15 May 1900). The Boer kraal position met a similar fate. They surrendered at the point of the bayonet just before dark.

With no Capt. Marsh to save them, however, other smaller and more isolated Boer groups trapped between the *stadt* and the river by the angry and vengeful Baralong were less fortunate. Pte Saunders had already observed terrible scenes of potential bloodlust as the hated Boers retreated:

> Many natives were having a ringside seat to watch the attack …
> They were on the verge of hysteria. They were jumping up and
> down, and stamping on the ground. At times their shrill yells
> could be heard during a lull in the firing. I'm sure they would
> have been happy to help us. They hated the Boers intensely.
> (Saunders, *Mafeking Memories*, p. 109)

Their 'ferocious help and the terrible fate of Boer stragglers has been left largely unrecorded by contemporary historians and even at the time kept secret, as the following description will reveal. After assessing the final Boer roll call of seventeen dead, 109 prisoners and nineteen wounded (out of a 300-strong force), Snyman wrote to enquire about another seventy men missing (ibid). In a description reminiscent of the 1838 Piet Retief massacre, when a sixty-strong Boer commando was butchered by the Zulu, Ross revealed their similarly horrendous fate:

> As a matter of fact our natives got amongst a small crowd of
> them in the native village and using their small wood-chopping
> axes soon made mincemeat of them and the pieces of them may
> now be found in the river. All this is, of course, kept private but
> it was said it was impossible to restrain the natives once they got
> amongst them, as they said they were only doing to the Boer
> what the Boers had done to them and their women. (ibid)

It is probable that Baden-Powell and other senior commanders also knew about these excesses, but, in the light of their professed beliefs in the concept of a 'gentlemen's war', as well as awareness of justified Baralong grievances, they would have been unwilling to publicise such an incident. A cryptic observation of the scenes in the aftermath of the battle, however, shows how Baden-Powell may well have known something of their fate. He noted: 'enemy's ambulance and search parties were out during the night picking-up in front of our outposts … our patrols reported blood spoor, arms and ammunition haversacks lying in quantities so that the losses had evidently been heavy' (Baden-Powell, 13 May 1900, Staff Diary, BPP). Baillie also spoke of up to 100 Boer bodies that 'will never be accounted for because the bodies of men with rifles may be possibly have been put away by the Baralongs' (Baillie, 15 May 1900, *Siege*, p. 265).

With the collapse of the Boer outposts in the *stadt*, the fate of the Boer-occupied BSAP fort was also not long delayed. Baillie noted how Eloff, the Boer commandant, had great difficulty in keeping his men together, with 100 men breaking away and escaping from the fort in spite of Eloff actually firing upon them. Hamilton, who was captured earlier during the struggle and incarcerated in the fort, reported on the final moments:

> Commandant Eloff called 'Surrender! Surrender!' and endeavoured strenuously to pacify his men. We upon our part shouted to the town to cease-fire; this was at once done whereupon the 67 Boers laid down their arms, handing them to the prisoners, who piled them up within the storehouse. Those of us who were not engaged in this work seized rifles and bandoliers from the heap and manned the defences of the fort until the prisoners could be delivered into proper custody. The Boers were then marched off and were found accommodation in the Masonic Hall and in the jail. (Hamilton, *Siege*, p. 309)

For some of the Mafeking inhabitants this deadly face-to-face confrontation with their Boer foe had been a revelatory and emotional experience. In Baillie's words:

> We had never before seen a dead or wounded Boer or a prisoner, and it is weary work to see your friends and neighbours shot and not to see your own bag too, but personally, except in the way of business, I hope I haven't killed a Boer. (Baillie, 15 May 1900, *Siege*, pp. 276–7)

For the many Boer prisoners the final surrender was itself a humiliating experience, as Baden-Powell assigned twenty Fingos 'to assist in guarding prisoners' and, while the 'Britishers marked a respectful silence … the natives however hooted' (ibid, p. 266).

There were clearly many black and white heroes in this final battle, but it is notable that several diarists, many of whom had been critical of other aspects of Baden-Powell's leadership, were united in their praise of his particular military performance. Thus Ross, while admitting that 'the other side of the man is open to much argument', paid a typically fulsome tribute:

> The morning of 12th [May] was, of course, the first opportunity any of us had had of seeing BP in a temporary corner or at all hard pressed. And I can assure you it was indeed a lesson to all who saw him. I had that luck. He stood there at the corner of his offices, the coolest of cucumbers possible, but his orders rattled out like the rip of a Maxim. He had taken in the position without a moment's thought or hesitation, and when he knew his outposts had been passed through by the enemy, within 20 minutes he had formed an inner line of defence right across the front of the town, with men and guns in sufficient numbers to mow down any number of the enemy that would dare to attempt to cross the clear open space still remaining between where the enemy were and the town. You could not realise his commands if put down in cold black and white. It was his tone, his self-possession, his command of self, his intimate knowledge of every detail of the defences, where everything at that moment was, and where it was to be brought and put to, showed us the ideal soldier, and what the British officer can be

and is in moments of extreme peril. It was something I would not have missed seeing for anything. With only one or two with him, his officers all galloping about delivering his orders, there he stood with his hands behind his back, a living image of a being knowing himself and his own strength and fearing neither foe nor devil. Such was BP the soldier. (Ross Diary, 16 May 1900)

AFTER THE BATTLE:
The Relief of Mafeking

The failed Eloff attack represented the Boers' 'last card' and was the fiercest engagement since the Game Tree Fort battle of December 1899. However, the strength, determination and ferocity of the Boer attack was a further testimony to how important Mafeking was perceived to be to them in military and, in particular, political terms. Five days later, the relief force at last arrived to a joyous welcome.

Officers of the Mafeking Relief Column. (Dr E.J. Yorke Collection)

In the intervening period, Mafeking eyewitnesses excitedly observed the steady evacuation by the Boers of their surrounding laagers and forts. Mr Algie noted the great excitement prevailing on 14 May as 'one large Boer group moved about the Southern Rise', the south-western Laager being 'vacated altogether' during the night (Algie Diary, 14 May 1900). As Col Mahon's 1,000-strong relief force closed in, Nurse Craufurd was moved to a more poetic observation: 'the great black mass by the laager seemed to divide itself and glide away in all directions and the veldt, before so quiet, was soon alive with horsemen' (Craufurd Diary, 17 May 1900).

Ecstatic scenes greeted the spearhead troops of Mahon's column, which had marched 250 miles in less than a fortnight, meeting Plumer about 7 miles west of Mafeking and 'absolutely confounding the Boers by their rapidity' (Wilson, *Memories*, p. 215). The first arrivals, a lead squadron of Imperial Light Horse

Brig. Gen. Bryan Thomas Mahon DSO. (Dr E.J. Yorke Collection)

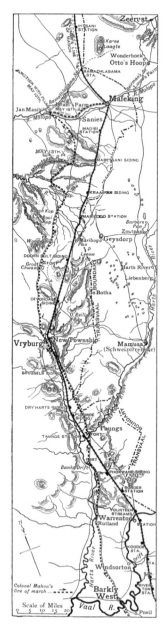

Map of the route of the flying column which relieved Mafeking. (Dr E.J. Yorke Collection)

Infantry under Maj. Kerri-Davis, received an initially muted welcome having arrived rapidly in the middle of the night and only after several false alarms. A greatly surprised Lady Wilson was one of the first to greet him in the gathering gloom as she was roused at her dinner by:

Some feeble cheers. Thinking something must have happened I ran to the market square and seeing a dusty khaki-clad figure whose appearance was unfamiliar to me, I touched him on the shoulder and said, 'Has anyone, come in?' 'We have come in,' he answered – Major Kerri-Davis and eight men of the Imperial Light Horse. Then I saw that officer himself and he told us that profiting by one hour's dusk they had ridden straight in before the moon rose and that they were now sending back two troopers to tell the column the way was clear. (Ibid)

Col Plumer's attempt to relieve Mafeking. (Dr E.J. Yorke Collection)

As word spread, however, these weary troopers were suddenly 'surrounded, besieged with questions, clapped upon the back, shaken by the hand and generally welcomed. Major Kerr-Davis called for cheers for the garrison while a crowd took up with tremendous fervour the National Anthem and Rule Britannia. It was an exciting moment and a picturesque scene bathed in soft moonlight and irradiated by the glow of countless stars'. (Hamilton, *Siege*, p. 315)

The main column's arrival a few hours later sparked off even wilder scenes of jubilation. Filson Young, an officer in the relief forces' lead units, described the highly emotional scenes as:

We galloped in over the trenches, past breastworks and redoubts and little forts until we pulled up at the door of the headquarters mess… No art could describe the handshaking and the welcome and the smiles on the faces of these tired-looking men; how they looked with rapt faces at us commonplace people from the outer world as though we were angels; how we all tried to speak at once, and only succeeded in gazing at each other and in saying, 'By jove!' 'Well I'm hanged!'

and the like senseless expressions that sometimes mean much to Englishmen. One man tried to speak then he swore; then he buried his face in his arms and sobbed. We all gulped at nothing, until someone brought in cocoa and we gulped that instead; then Baden-Powell came in, and one could only gaze at him and search in vain on his jolly face for the traces of seven months' anxiety and strain. (Filson Young, *Relief of Mafeking*, pp. 264–5)

It was a night noisily celebrated by the black citizens of Mafeking who had contributed so much to the survival of the garrison. In her hospital Nurse Craufurd was kept wide awake listening 'to the noise of the Baralongs celebrating the relief. Poor creatures, they had suffered fearfully during these seven and a half months, but had been loyal and brave through all' (Craufurd Diary, 17 May 1900). As the main relief column arrived, the real celebrations began. Hamilton again provides a vivid description of the scenes of jubilation:

About two in the morning a subdued roar came from the direction of the north-west outposts and, in a very little time word was passed round that the troops were making their entrance into Mafeking. The town had aroused itself and was soon flocking across the veldt to the ground where the combined columns had already begun to form their camp. It was not a large force; its full muster was below 2,000; but amid the soft and eerie shadows of the starry, moonlit night, there seemed no end to the lines of horses, mules, and bullocks, to the camp fires, to the groups of men, to the number and variety of the wagons. In a corner, as it were, were the guns, a composite battery of the Royal Horse Artillery, eight pieces of the Canadian Artillery, and a number of maxims. It was these, which we had heard booming to us the first distant echoes of relief, and we were, of course, proud of them. Then and there we examined them, felt them over, pondered upon them, and then and there

Lt Smitheman of the Rhodesian Regiment, who got through the Boer lines into Mafeking and returned with reports to Col Plumer. (Dr E.J. Yorke Collection)

we thanked our god that we had in our own hands at least some really serviceable artillery. But there were other sights to be seen, early as was the hour, tired as were the troopers. There were the men of the Kimberley Light Horse and their comrades of the Imperial Light Horse to be inspected, to be patted upon the back, to be admired, and to be congratulated. Everyone seemed to be screaming, and as the Royal Horse Artillery swept through town we streamed after them, feebly endeavouring to keep pace with them, so as to be able to witness the effect of their power. The Market Square at this time presented a picture of military life that has never been equalled by any of the scenes that have been enacted there in its early days. Men in uniform were hurrying from point to point, troops from the various squadrons were coming in, squadron leaders, majors and colonels were falling over one another … (Hamilton, *Siege*, pp. 315–7)

Not all of Mafeking's rescuers behaved as correctly as might have been expected. The 16-year-old Rifleman Saunders again recalled:

Yes, they were a fine bunch of soldiers but part of their training must have been shoplifting. They were souvenir crazy and had to have a memento of the Defence of Mafeking. We found this out too late. They took everything loose … After our visitors had gone, I missed my puttees, hat and tunic … I treasured the hat because of the bullet hole through the looped up hat brim. (Saunders, *Mafeking*, p. 119)

Contrary to some of his critics, Baden-Powell had not been inactive during these final days and hours. As news arrived on 15 May of 500 Boers posted to 'receive Plumer's force', he prepared a small column of 220 men (including units of the Protectorate Regiment, BSAP, Cape Police and Bechuanaland Rifles) and two guns and a Maxim under Col Wexford 'to take the offensive; if necessary to create a diversion to help our relief' (Baden-Powell, 15 May 1900, Staff Diary, BPP).

Artillery in Mafeking waiting to cooperate with the relief column. (Dr E.J. Yorke Collection)

Mafeking Medical Facilities:

Victoria Hospital: seventy beds and Base Hospital
Major Anderson, Royal Army Medical
Corps and Principal Medical Officer
Dr W. Hayes (acted as Principal Medical Officer for first
part of siege)
Surgeon-Major Holmden, British South Africa
Police
Dr T. Hayes, District Surgeon
Dr Elmes

The arrival of the Canadian Artillery and their shelling of Game Tree Fort had in fact proved the final straw for the residual defending Boer forces. The shelling continued for an hour, led by the composite battalion of the Royal Horse Artillery's four 12½lb guns and two pom-poms, and culminated in both garrison and relief forces advancing in skirmishing order. Lines were extended rapidly until Boer positions were out-flanked. In their rush to escape, even the Boer hospital and headquarters were abandoned, leaving thirty Boer wounded to their fate. Perhaps showing awareness of what had earlier happened to their Boer

The meeting of Baden-Powell and Mahon. (Dr E.J. Yorke Collection)

comrades at the hands of the vengeful Baralong, Baden-Powell hastily posted a guard around the hospital. Game Tree Fort had been abandoned earlier, the Imperial guns 'terrorising the Boers' who 'fled precipitately, leaving their camp, their guns, their stores, behind them' (Hamilton, *Siege*, p. 318).

It was the signal for a mass plunder of the Boer camps by white and black, civilian and military alike. An astonished Lady Wilson 'had the

The Relief of Mafeking: the procession through the market square.
(Dr E.J. Yorke Collection)

experience of seeing a "loot" in progress. First we saw two soldiers driving a cow; then some more with bulged-out pockets full of live fowls; natives were staggering under huge loads of food stuffs, and eating them as they walked!' (Wilson, *Memories*, p. 218). Whole wagon loads of Boer food were ransacked as if to compensate for the terrible past months of virtual starvation. Baden-Powell himself gazed upon 'several wagon loads of food stuffs and ammunition abandoned with all the Boer trenches hurriedly evacuated and food, clothing, arms, blankets etc., left behind in profusion' (Baden-Powell, 13 May 1900, Staff Diary). McMullen's camp became a special target and was duly 'searched for food and souvenirs of the Boers' (Algie Diary, 18 May 1900). A half-starved Rifleman Saunders recalled his own experience on entering a recently abandoned Boer trench, having earlier witnessed, by telescope, the frantic confusion within the Boer laager with:

> wagons hitching up, other wagons and riders going east without any resemblance of military formation. It was a rout! … For a moment I didn't realise what I was doing. Then I was at it myself, picking up stale bread crusts, half-chewed strips, of biltong, and fragments of "fat cookies", both off the floor and from chinks of the sandbags – we had cleaned up everything edible. (Saunders, *Mafeking Memories*, p. 117)

Leading citizens were not averse to acquiring private loot. Ross himself took a return 6-mile walk to the Boer main laager to get his share of the booty:

> We went out and we came back loaded down with all sorts of good things. I managed to secure myself a bag of flour and my pockets were crammed full of biltong, a flask of whiskey found under one of the beds and a lot of other curios. Quite enough to carry for a three mile tramp home again! (Ross Diary, 20 May 1900)

As the looting subsided, time was made for the more sombre task of paying respects to the dead and offering thanksgiving. On 19 May, the whole garrison paraded at the cemetery where, after a ceremony conducted by the Reverend Weeks, a Protectorate Regiment firing party fired three volleys over the graves of their dead comrades. A thanksgiving service was also held, Baden-Powell speaking personally to each detachment in turn. On this day the Town Guard was officially disbanded.

The Mafeking celebrations were mirrored, indeed far surpassed, by the ecstatic reaction at home. The whole country dissolved into a delirium of joyfulness, the grand 'Mafficking', thus adding a new word to the English language. After the desperately gloomy events of the last seven months, only temporarily relieved by the British victory at Paardeberg in February 1900, the relief had unleashed a cathartic explosion of emotion affecting all classes of people and practically every town and village in Britain. As *The Times* confirmed on Saturday 19 May 1900: 'by common consent a public holiday

The first train into Mafeking. Its passage through the veldt had been disguised with foliage as far as possible. (Dr E.J. Yorke Collection)

Mafeking Day at Piccadilly Circus. The announcement of the Relief of Mafeking was made somewhat unconventionally by an excited footman at the Mansion House at 9.35 p.m. on 18 May 1900. (Dr E.J. Yorke Collection)

had arranged itself' (*The London Times*, 21 May 1900). It underlined how important Mafeking had become as a psychological symbol, a veritable beacon of hope for the British Empire, far beyond its intrinsic military value. Just as the heroic defence of Rorke's Drift (in which an unprecedented eleven VCs were awarded) compensated for the earlier disaster to British arms at Isandlwana, and the victory at Omdurman substituted for the fall of Khartoum and the death of Gen. Gordon, so the Relief of Mafeking made up for the earlier devastating military blunders of 'Black Week'.

Never before in Britain's history had such a wave of patriotic hysteria swept the nation, and not even the Armistice of 1918 or VE Day in 1945 were equal to the scale and extent of the celebration. Within five minutes of the news arriving at 9.17 p.m. on 18 May, crowds of up to 20,000 surrounded the Mansion House in London singing the National Anthem. The frantic Saturday scenes were described by one eyewitness:

> White-haired old ladies were to be seen carrying large union jacks in each hand, and young women had colours pinned across from shoulder to shoulder. Sober-looking young men

in spectacles stood at street corners blowing tin trumpets with all their might… Well-dressed young women of unusually proper demeanour traversed roadways, arm-in-arm, six abreast, carrying flags and occasionally bursting into song. There was a singular absence of any official stimulus. (ibid)

The spontaneity of the response was graphically illustrated by scenes even within the normally sedate Stock Exchange, the financial powerhouse of empire. The work of both members and clerks was abandoned as groups shook hands, singing patriotic songs and the National Anthem with much fervour. Such euphoria was repeated all over the British Empire. In Canada, a correspondent reported that 'every town and village went wild with patriotic fever'. In Melbourne, Australia, guns were fired, bells rang all day and crowds packed the streets. In the midst of all the celebrations Baden-Powell emerged as the greatest British hero since Wellington and Nelson. It was five days before the country was able to return to normal. (For a voluminous extended discussion of the 'mafficking' celebrations in Britain and throughout the British Empire, see Gardner, *Mafeking*, pp. 199–207.)

Back in South Africa, 'Mafficking' was taking a far more sinister form as, in the aftermath of the siege, the black defenders of Mafeking and their local allies proceeded to exact a swift revenge on both the retreating Boer commandos and their African allies. For a brief while, all of Snyman's and Cronje's earlier expressed fears and the nightmare scenario of a 'racial Armageddon' seemed close to realisation. As the Mafeking garrison's white citizens continued to celebrate, armed raiding parties of Baralong, many undoubtedly equipped with Mauser rifles captured from the Boers during the Eloff attack and the post-relief orgy of looting, rapidly moved out of the town to seek retribution. An early primary target was the rebel Baralong chief Abraham Metuba's village at Rietfontein. He had actively supported the Boers during the siege and allegedly killed several of the garrison's messengers. On 19 May, a band of 300 Mafeking Baralongs, led by Wessels, duly raided Metuba's kraal, looting all his cattle, with Metuba and fifteen of his headmen captured and brought in to be jailed. A trusty ally, the headman Saani, imprisoned by Metuba's pro-Boer group, was simultaneously rescued (Baillie, 15 May 1900, p. 284). Baillie mused on this unusual situation and welcomed the rough justice meted out to these 'black traitors':

> I suppose this is the first occasion in which one black man surrendered under a white flag to another. These Rietsfontein rebels have always been against the remainder of the Baralongs, and have invariably fought for the Boers since the disturbed relations between Briton and Boer have existed. I hope they will shoot Metuba, as his people's invariable cunning in stopping our runners has caused us great inconvenience, not to mention the numbers they have killed. (Baillie, 17 May 1900, *Siege*, p. 285)

Black on black violence was one thing, but uncontrolled violence by armed blacks against whites, which escalated to the killing of the largely defenceless Boers on outlying farms, inevitably forced the imperial authorities to intervene, if only to defend white order. By the end of May it was clear that the profusion of armed African bands in the region was posing a serious threat to overall white authority. As local Boers pleaded for protection, Baden-Powell himself was forced to act against his own black allies. On 26 May he accordingly instructed Col Plumer to formerly warn the hitherto friendly Chief Linchwe 'that he must on no account invade Marico and that, if the Boers at Sequan wanted to surrender, he would assure their protection' (Baden-Powell to Plumer, 26 May 1900, Mafeking Archives, hereafter abbreviated to MA). On the same day, Cols Plumer, Edwards and Gould-Adams were formally ordered to not only take the surrender of local Boers, but also to provide them with protection against 'natives invading the Transvaal' (Baden-Powell to Plumer, Edwards and Gould-Adams, ibid). Three days later, on 29 May, Chiefs Linchwe and Kalifing were directly 'warned to restrain

The mustering of Plumer's volunteers at Bulawayo. (Dr E.J. Yorke Collection)

Brig. Gen. Herbert C.O. Plumer. (Dr E.J. Yorke Collection)

their men from looting' (Algie Diary, 29 May 1900). Racial clashes and confrontations soon escalated.

By 31 May the panicking Landdrost (magistrate) at Lichtenburg had urgently requested Baden-Powell to take over the district as '100 armed natives were marching on the town' (ibid, 31 May 1900). As the 'racial genie' slowly emerged out of its lamp, British and Boers alike were forced to hastily form a temporary 'unholy alliance' to forestall a general race war.

By early June 1900, Baden-Powell had been reluctantly forced into carrying out a sustained campaign of pacification and 'reconquest', not only of his main Boer enemy and their African allies, but his own armed African auxiliaries. On 2 June, Baden-Powell ominously reported to Gen. Roberts that, while supplies were now plentiful, the 'only difficulties for the moment are bands of armed natives marauding' for which he was 'taking repressive measures'. (Baden-Powell to Roberts, 2 June 1900, MA). By 4 June it was reported that 'serious looting was taking place at Barberspan by Mafeking Baralongs'. The wider political ramifications of this local racial crisis was soon evident, with the South African High Commissioner himself now becoming 'very anxious about the matter'. (Mahon to Baden-Powell, 4 June 1900, MA) Consequently, Baden-Powell ordered the local Baralongs to hand in all arms and to return to their kraals with Chief Lekoko once again told to warn his people.

Near Lichtenburg, thirty 'looting Baralongs' were apprehended by British Gen. Hunter, and Baden-Powell was soon forced to establish small posts of troops throughout the country, while mounted police on commandeered horses were dispersed about the border to stop the raiding and looting. It was not, however, a policy of all-out repression. Baden-Powell privately expressed considerable sympathy for the Baralong grievances and demonstrated his acute awareness of their previous loyal service.

Col. Hore's fort, captured by Eloff. (Dr E.J. Yorke Collection)

On 19 June, for instance, he recommended to Lord Roberts that 'a reward be made to the Baralong Chiefs for their loyalty and good service in the shape of 100 head of cattle to Chief Lekoko as well as to Chiefs Silas, Molema and Paul Manip' (Baden-Powell to Roberts, 19 June 1900, MA). It was a policy actively supported by his grateful fellow Mafeking citizens. Baillie reflected on the Baralong plight and expressed deep sympathy for the reasons lying behind their attacks on the Boer farms:

> I wonder if people at home realise in what position our loyalists in Bechuanaland have been placed. If they didn't come in their own countrymen regarded them as rebels – if they did, they lost all they had. But by doing as they have done, that is by carrying on their business while exposed to all the contumely and insult the Boers could heap on them, with the possible loss of life as well as property they have served their country as well as those who have taken up arms; because their houses have always been a safe place for runners to go to, and news about the doings of the Boers could be obtained from them. Besides, they know which of the Boers fought, and which didn't, and this fact now terrifies the rebels and keeps many quiet, who might not otherwise be so. (Baillie, 17 May 1900, *Siege*, p. 285)

Other leading 'Mafekingites', in addition to Baden-Powell and Baillie, also participated in this 'carrot and stick' policy of pacification. Thus, Weil, the Mafeking supply merchant, personally delivered 200 bags of mealies 'to his friends the Baralong' (ibid, 19 May 1900). Raiding expeditions soon diminished, with Chief Linchwe being one of the last Baralong chiefs to be contained – but not until his 'war parties', furiously raiding cattle near Pilandsberg, 30 miles north, had 'killed one Boer boy and wounded two others' (Baden-Powell to Roberts, 23 June 1900, MA).

Thus, by the end of June all-out racial conflict had been narrowly averted as 4,000 Boer rifles and 1,000 'native guns' were confiscated by Baden-Powell's troops. Lord Roberts thus confirmed that the wholesale disarmament of the Transvaal African population had been 'absolutely necessary else unarmed Boers not safe' (Roberts to Baden-Powell, 27 June 1900, MA). As racial order was rapidly restored, Roberts added, with evident relief: 'We find in practice natives giving in arms quite willingly and the measure highly approved of by both Boer and British farmers' (ibid). This disarmament of the Baralong had certainly taxed the imperial conscience, already acutely aware of their overall loyalty during the siege and the brutal provocation they had received from the Boer besieging forces. As the High Commissioner had earlier informed Lord Roberts prior to disarmament:

I have informed Mafeking that orders have been given for Linchwe people to be disarmed. I hope it may not be thought necessary to carry out this step, as it is totally contrary to the policies successfully pursued by myself and all my predecessors with regard to the Protectorate natives who are directly under the High Commissioner. The present is, I think, a particularly unfortunate time for such a step as the Protectorate natives … have been most loyal during the war and have greatly assisted us. (British High Commissioner South Africa to Roberts, enclosed in Roberts to Baden-Powell, 25 June 1900, MA)

The aftermath of the siege, as much as the siege itself, had therefore been of significant political consequence, with a short-lived but direct African challenge to local colonial order. In a sense, this brief exhibition of African 'independence' had been realised only through their extensive sacrifices during the Siege of Mafeking. In the event, the Official History of South Africa's total casualty roll for Mafeking belied the extent of their losses: sixty-five 'natives' and 264 Baralongs were listed as killed or died of wounds, but to this figure, of course, must be added the several hundred African civilians who died from malnutrition or disease. Total white combatant losses were listed as sixty-seven, with the black contingents losing twenty-five. The total civilian and military casualties, wounded, killed and missing, during the siege were officially listed as 813 of all races (HMG, Official History of the War in South Africa, vol. 2, p. 550). Such statistics, however, ignored the clearly immense psychological pressures endured by both black and white Mafeking citizens during this epic seven and a half month siege.

THE LEGACY

The political and military importance of the Siege of Mafeking has been significantly underestimated. In military terms it can be argued that the siege did, in fact, create a major diversion of existing Boer forces and significantly undermined its early war effort. The siege initially tied down up to 8,000 Boer combatants, which constituted up to one-fifth of the total existing Boer armed strength in the autumn of 1899. Even after Cronje's departure in November and the significant reduction in the size of the besieging force, many more Boer patrols had to be continuously deployed to protect their farms against constant garrison raids which extended up to a 30-mile radius. The garrison at Mafeking proved to be a running sore in the 'body politic' of the Transvaal Boer authorities.

The siege was of even greater significance in psychological terms. As even Thomas Pakenham, an otherwise severe critic of Baden-Powell, has pointed out: 'Wars are ultimately about morale.' Baden-Powell and his resolute garrison had scored a great victory, as they had 'not only given back Britain its self-confidence, but dealt the Boers a crushing psychological blow by denying them Mafeking, the symbolic birthplace of the Raid. No other British commander in the war had done so much with so little' (Pakenham, *Boer War*, p. 417). The unprecedented scenes of celebration throughout Britain, following a litany of imperial disaster, were a glowing testament of this irrefutable fact.

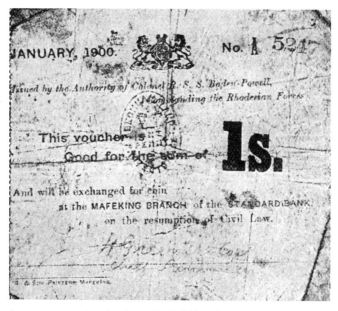

Paper currency printed and used in Mafeking. (Dr E.J. Yorke Collection)

Mafeking siege stamp made in the town. (Dr E.J. Yorke Collection)

Baden-Powell emerged as a high-calibre military leader and this was demonstrated clearly by his tactical handling of the Eloff attack, an achievement universally admired by his contemporaries. Similarly, there is no substantial evidence of Baden-Powell's alleged homosexuality; his friendships with several officers, such as Hazelrigg, were clearly based on often long-standing military comradeship in the midst of considerable adversity.

In other ways the siege was an important political watershed turning point in the course of the Anglo-Boer War. What had begun as an ostensibly 'white man's war' had, confirming local Boer fears, rapidly developed into a multi-racial conflict with, as we have seen, serious implications for the post-siege, indeed possibly post-war, social order. In the early weeks of the siege, Baden-Powell had happily played the 'race card' in order to demoralise his Boer opponents. It was therefore perhaps ironic that he himself was to be haunted by the appearance of the dreaded 'black spectre' during the troublesome weeks following the ending of the siege. Some form of black challenge was perhaps inevitable. African siege heroes, often sharing equal rations and military duties with their white counterparts, revelled in this new enhanced social status.

As early as January 1900, the logistical dependency of the white garrison upon their African collaborators and auxiliaries had become patently evident. Baralong livestock raids had been matched by the courageous activities of the African unarmed and

Cape of Good Hope postage stamps. (Dr E.J. Yorke Collection)

armed auxiliaries such as the Cape Boys, who played a crucial role in the defence of key areas of Mafeking, such as the Brickfields defence line. J.A. Hamilton, the war correspondent, paid fulsome tribute to the local Baralong community who, in the later stages of the siege, constituted a vital garrison lifeline:

> In a way we have been compelled to depend to no small extent upon the prowess of the local tribe. The Baralong have done well by us, and have served us faithfully, and with no complaint. They have fought for us; they have preyed upon the enemy's cattle so that the white garrison might have something better than horse flesh for their diet; they have manned the western defences of the Stadt and they have suffered severe privations with extraordinary fortitude. (Hamilton, *Siege*, p. 261)

While some Africans had politically and even economically prospered as a result of the siege, there were also, of course, many less fortunate African 'victims'. As we have seen, several hundred Africans perished from starvation and/or disease during the siege period, particularly the months of January to March. While the ignorance, neglect and belated relief policies of the white authorities played a significant role in this tragedy, inter-ethnic rivalry in the form of Baralong exclusivity cannot be discounted as a factor in exacerbating the food crisis. While many of the itinerant Transvaal African refugee groups faced starvation, many of their established Baralong counterparts survived, even prospered, maintaining sizable cattle herds and vegetable gardens through to the final days of the siege.

This immensely contentious issue of African welfare brings us to a re-assessment of the role of the man in charge, Lord Baden-Powell. During his conduct of the Siege of Mafeking, Baden-Powell, like many military leaders, was forced to take many harsh political decisions, of which the policy of the enforced evacuation of 'alien' African groups remains the most controversial. It was never simply a brutal policy of 'leave or starve', as Baden-Powell was under immense psychological and military pressures outside his immediate control. His meticulous rationing plans were completely undermined by the telegraphed news received from Lord Roberts in February, and again in early April, significantly delaying relief.

The policy of evacuation was high risk, but the success of earlier voluntary evacuations would have given him some hope for success. Moreover, he did make genuine attempts to mitigate any adverse effects of this exodus, providing both armed escorts and food supplies for the evacuees, as well as seeking Boer guarantees for their safe passage. In hindsight it was a blunder, but was the product of Baden-Powell's naivety and misjudgement rather than any concept of premeditated murder as recent critics have seemed to suggest.

After the disaster of the February exodus, Baden-Powell never repeated an enforced mass evacuation policy again. Furthermore, he made positive efforts over the next two months to alleviate cases of acute starvation amongst the remaining Transvaal African groups, not only through his soup kitchen system, but also by *direct* interventions such as the rescue and feeding of up to fifty starving Shangaanis on 15 April. On 21 April he even held a crisis meeting almost solely concerned with the problem of African food supplies, and which resulted in directives to improve the quality and nutritious value of the kitchen soup supplies. Furthermore, he frequently rewarded African cattle raiders and soldiers. These were not the actions of a 'war criminal'. Even radical contemporary critics such as Neilly gave him credit for extensive remedial measures taken after the extent of the African food crisis had become clear.

Moreover, as Hamilton and other contemporary eyewitnesses have observed, Baden-Powell was an exceptionally busy man, preoccupied, if not obsessed, with the garrison defences and military matters in general. He rarely visited the African *stadt* or soup kitchen areas and spent most of his time either in his headquarters office or 'look-out position', or surveying the

A street traverse in Mafeking showing a corrugated iron barricade similar to that which held Eloff in check. (Dr E.J. Yorke Collection)

external defence areas by night and day. African welfare was invariably left to subordinates to organise and administer.

Indeed, it is clear that malpractices and irregularities were carried out by some junior officers and officials, who were both controlling the soup kitchens and involved in the requisition of food. The more humanitarian Col Hore, on at least one occasion, drew attention to this continuing problem at the lower levels of administration, and Plaatje himself made several cryptic and overt references to such junior administrators and their overall ignorance or intolerance of African customs and welfare needs. As Plaatje tellingly observed, the African supply arrangements were 'in the hands of young officers who know as little about natives and their mode of living as they know about the man on the moon and his mode of living' (Plaatje, Mafeking Diary, p. 80). Much has also been made of the African executions which occurred during the siege, but these tragedies, spread over a seven and a half month period, were comparatively rare and were not personally administered by Baden-Powell. The Court of Summary Jurisdiction was also invariably run by other senior officers.

If at times he was excessively harsh in his policies towards elements of the African population, he could at times be equally severe towards the white community. White deserters were sentenced to death in absentia and would have been shot if caught. His decision to move Dutch women and children into the line of Boer shellfire in January provides another example of this. Indeed, some of the more extreme attacks launched against him by his white critics were, if not motivated by envy, were at least partly based on growing resentment at his increasingly authoritarian control over the *European* garrison. All the war correspondents, Mr Ross and even Mr Algie, had clashed with Baden-Powell on separate occasions. If in overall terms his racial sympathies ultimately lay with the white community, it was surely a not unexpected reflection of the prevailing racial prejudices of his time – he was stereotypical of his generation.

Notwithstanding this fact, the tragic deaths which occurred within Mafeking still pale into insignificance when compared with the newly discovered large-scale black 'concentration camps' set up later in the Anglo-Boer War and, indeed, the enforced incarceration of thousands of *white* women and children in such camps under the 'scorched earth' policy of Lord Roberts and Gen. Kitchener. Such policies were to cost many more thousands of lives across the racial divide.

In summary, Lord Baden-Powell's policies during the Siege of Mafeking were no harsher, indeed arguably even less harsh, than the policies of many of his contemporaries towards African communities during the Anglo-Boer War. Like all prominent leaders, Baden-Powell had his faults – he could be vain, egotistical and, on occasions, stubborn and uncompromising – but his actions were invariably conditioned by military exigencies *not* by conscious or deliberate racism.

ORDER OF BATTLE

Mafeking Garrison (Cmdr: Col R.S. Baden-Powell)

	Officers	Men
Protectorate Regiment (Lt Col Hore)	21	448
BSAP (Lt Col Walford)	10	81
Cape Police (Inspectors Marsh and Browne)	4	99
Bechuanaland Rifles (Capt. Cowan)	5	77
The Town Guard (Maj., local Lt Col Vyvyan)	6	296
Railway Detachment (Capt. Moore)	1	115
Cape Boy Contingent/Corps (Cmdt Lord Edward Cecil)	67	

Total: 1,230

Besieging Boer Forces
October to November 1899 (Cmdr: Gen. P. Cronje)
Up to 8,000 men, drawn from various Transvaal commandos

November 1899 to May 1900 (Cmdr: Gen. J.P. Snyman)
Up to 2,000 men

FURTHER READING

Recommended Archives: National Army Museum, London;
National Archives, Kew, London; British Museum, London;
Rhodes House Library, Oxford; Mafeking Museum Archives,
Mafeking, South Africa.

Select Bibliography

Aitken, W.F., *Baden-Powell: The Hero of Mafeking* (Partridge and
    Co., 1900)
Baden-Powell, Colonel R.S.S., *Lessons from the Varsity of Life*
    (Pearson, 1933)
–– *Sketches in Mafeking and East Africa* (Smith Elder, 1980)
Baden-Powell, Lady Olave and Hillcourt, W., *Baden-Powell: Two
    Lives of a Hero* (Heinemann, 1964)
Baillie, F.D., *Mafeking: A Diary of the* Siege (Constable, 1980)
Beghie, H., *The Wolf that Never Sleeps* (Richards, 1900)
Bennett, I., *A Rain of Lead: The Siege and Surrender of
    Potchefstroom* (Greenhill, 2001)
Bremner Smith, R.J., *Colonel R.S.S. Baden-Powell* (London, 1900)
Fletcher, J.S., *Baden-Powell of Mafeking* (Methuen, 1900)
Flower-Smith, M., and Yorke, E.J., *Mafeking: The Story of a Siege*
    (Covos Day, 2000)
Gardner, B., *Mafeking: A Victorian Legend* (Cassell, 1965)

Godley, R.S., *Khaki and Blue* (Lovat, Dickson and Thompson, 1935)

Godley, Sir A., *Life of an Irish Soldier* (John Murray, 1939)

Grinnell-Milne, D., *Baden-Powell at Mafeking* (Bodley Head, 1957)

Hamilton, J.A., *The Siege of Mafeking* (Methuen, 1900)

HMSO, *The Boer War: Ladysmith and Mafeking* (London, 1999)

Hopkins, P. and Dungmore, H., *The Boy: Baden-Powell and the Siege of Mafeking* (Zebra Books, 1999)

Jeal, T., *Baden*-Powell (Hutchinson, 1989)

Kiernan, R.H., *Baden-Powell* (Harrap, 1939)

Midgley, J.F., *Petticoat in Mafeking: The Letters of Ada Cock* (Cape Town, 1974)

Neilly, J., *Besieged with BP* (Pearson, 1900)

Reynolds, E.E., *Baden-Powell* (Oxford, 1942)

Rosenthal, M., *The Character Factory* (Collins and Sons, 1986)

Smuts, J.C., *Jan Christian Smuts by his Son* (Cassell, 1952)

Saunders, F., *Mafeking Memories*, P. Thurmond Smith (ed.), (London Associated University Press,1996)

Stirling, J., *The* Colonials *in South Africa* (Blackwood, 1907)

Whalley, G.F., *With Plumer to Mafeking* (London, 1900)

Willan, B., *Edward Ross: Diary of the Siege of Mafeking* (Cape Town, 1980)

Wade, E.K., *The Piper of Pax* (Pearson, 1924)

Wilson, H.W. (ed.), *With the Flag to Pretoria, vols 1 and 2* (Harmsworth, 1901)

Plaatje, Sol T., *Mafeking Diary* (Meridor Books, 1973)

Wilson, Lady Sarah, *South African Memories* (Arnold, 1909)

Young, F., *The Relief of Mafeking* (Methuen, 1900)

Key General and Unit Histories

Amery, L.S. (ed.), *The Times History of the War in South Africa,* vols 2 and 4 (London Times, 1900–04)

Carver, Field Marshal Lord, *The National Army Museum Book of the Boer War* (Sidgwick and Jackson, 1999)

Conan Doyle, A., *The Great Boer War* (Smith, Elder and Co., 1901)

Featherstone, D., *Weapons and Equipment of the Victorian Soldier* (Blandford Press, 1978)

Hamilton, Gen. Sir Ian, *Listening for the Drums* (London, 1944)

Harding, C., *Frontier Patrols: History of the BSA Police* (Bell, 1937)

Headley, C. (ed.), *The Milner Papers, vols 1 and 2* (London and South Africa, 1899–1905, and vol. 2, 1931–35)

Kruger, R., *Goodbye Dolly Gray: A History of the Boer War* (Cassell, 1959)

Le May, G.H., *British Supremacy in South Africa, 1899–1907* (Oxford, 1965)

Nasson, W., *The South African War, 1899–1902* (Arnold, 1899)

Pakenham, E., *Jameson's Raid* (Wiedenfield and Nicholson, 1960)

Pakenham T., *The Boer War* (Wiedenfield and Nicholson, 1979)

Spiers, E., *The Army and Society, 1815–1914* (London, 1980)

Warwick, P. (ed.), *Black People and the South African War* (CUP, 1983)

Yorke, E.J., *Forgotten Colonial Crisis: Britain and Northern Rhodesia at War, 1914–18* (Palgrave/Macmillan, 2014)

Key Articles/Unpublished Papers

Baden-Powell, R.S.S., Staff Diary (NAM)

Bennett, I., '*Supply and Transport in the Boer War, 1899–1902*' (*Soldiers of the Queen*, issue 87, December 1996)

Renew, A., Algie Diary (Mafeking Archives)

Newspapers and Periodicals

The London Times, 1899–1900

The Illustrated London News, 1899–1900

The Graphic, 1899–1900

Black and White Magazine, 1899–1900

Crompton's Magazine (notably, Craufurd, A.M., 'A Nurse's Diary', C.M., 1900)

INDEX

Index